AQA

GCSE Mathematics
Modular

Sue Chandler   Ewart Smith

Higher

Module 3

Heinemann Educational Publishers
Halley Court, Jordan Hill, Oxford OX2 8EJ
Part of Harcourt Education

Heinemann is the registered trademark of Harcourt Education Limited

© Text Sue Chandler, Ewart Smith

First published 2006

10 09 08 07 06
10 9 8 7 6 5 4 3 2 1

British Library Cataloguing in Publication Data is available from the British Library on request.
10-digit ISBN: 0 435807 22 6
13-digit ISBN: 978 0 435807 22 1

The right of Sue Chandler and Ewart Smith to be identified as joint authors of this book has been asserted by them in accordance with the Copyright, Designs and Patents Act 1998.

Edited by Carol Harris
Designed by Wooden Ark Studios
Typeset by Tech-Set Ltd, Gateshead, Tyne and Wear

Original illustrations © Harcourt Education Limited, 2006
Illustrated by Phil Garner
Cover design mccdesign ltd
Printed in the United Kingdom by Scotprint

Cover photo: Digital Vision ©
Consultant examiners: David Pritchard, Andy Darbourne
Series editor: Harry Smith

Acknowledgements
Harcourt Education Ltd would like to thank those schools who helped in the development and trialling of this course.

The author and publisher would like to thank the following individuals and organisations for permission to reproduce photographs:
Corbis pp **2**, **10**, **65**, **73**, **82**, **99**; Alamy Images/Neil McAllister pp **20**; Photos.com pp **28**, **52**, **56**; iStockPhoto pp **6**, **79**; NASA pp **79**; Corbis/Charles O'Rear pp **81**; Getty Images/ PhotoDisc pp **82**; Alamy Images/Mike Stone pp **93**; Alamy Images/Enigma pp **104**; MorgueFile/Daniele Musella pp **120**; Richard Smith pp **124**; Science Photo Library/Takeshi Takahara pp **128**

Every effort has been made to contact copyright holders of material reproduced in this book. Any omissions will be rectified in subsequent printings if notice is given to the publishers.

Publishing team

Editorial	Design/Production	Picture research
Sarah Flockhart	Christopher Howson	Chrissie Martin
Maggie Rumble	Phil Leafe	
Joanna Shock	Helen McCreath	

There are links to relevant websites in this book. In order to ensure that the links are up-to-date, that the links work , and that sites are not inadvertently linked to sites that could be considered offensive, we have made the links available on the Heinemann website at www.heneimann.co.uk/hotlinks. When you access the site, the express code is 7226P.

Tel: 01865 888058   www.heinemann.co.uk   www.tigermaths.co.uk

How to use this book

This book is designed to give you the best possible preparation for your AQA GCSE Module 3 Examination. The authors are experienced writers of successful school mathematics textbooks and each book has been exactly tailored to your GCSE maths specification.

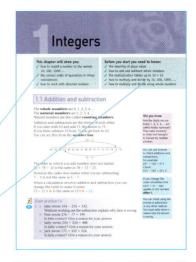

Finding your way around

To help you find your way around when you are studying and revising use the

- **contents list** – this gives a detailed breakdown of the topics covered in each chapter
- **list of objectives** at the start of each chapter – this tells you what you will learn in the chapter
- **list of prerequisite knowledge** at the start of each chapter – this tells you what you need to know before starting the chapter
- **index** – on page 151 – you can use this to find any topic covered in this book.

Remembering key facts

At the end of each chapter you will find

- **a summary of key points** – this lists the key facts and techniques covered in the chapter
- **grade descriptions** – these tell you which techniques and skills most students need to be able to use to achieve each exam grade
- **a glossary** – this gives the definitions of the mathematical words used in the chapter.

Exercises and practice papers

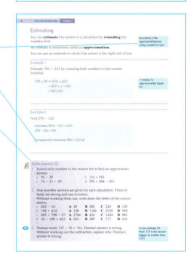

- **Worked examples** show you exactly how to answer exam questions.
- **Tips and hints** highlight key techniques and explain the reasons behind the answers.
- **Exam practice** questions work from the basics up to exam level. Hints and tips help you achieve your highest possible grade.
- The icon **A01** against a question is Using and Applying mathematics. These questions ask you to give reasons for your answers
- **An examination practice paper** on page 136 helps you prepare for your written examination.
- **Answers** for all the questions are included at the end of the book.

Coursework, communication and technology

- **Mini coursework tasks** throughout the book will help you practice the skills needed for your GCSE coursework tasks.
- **ICT tasks** will highlight opportunities to use computer programs and the Internet to help your understanding of mathematical topics.
- **Class discussion** sections allow you to talk about problems and what techniques you might use to solve them.

Contents

5 Approximation and estimation

6 Indices and standard form

7 Measures

8 Percentages

9 Algebra and graphs

10 Ratio and proportion

1 Integers

This chapter will show you:	Before you start you need to know:
✓ how to round a number to the nearest 10, 100, 1000 …	✓ the meaning of place value
✓ the correct order of operations in mixed calculations	✓ how to add and subtract whole numbers
✓ how to work with directed numbers	✓ the multiplication tables up to 10×10
	✓ how to multiply and divide by 10, 100, 1000, …
	✓ how to multiply and divide using whole numbers

1.1 Addition and subtraction

The **whole numbers** are 0, 1, 2, 3, 4, …
The **natural numbers** are 1, 2, 3, 4, …
Natural numbers are also called **counting numbers**.

Addition and subtraction are the inverse of each other.
If you start with 63 and add 12, the answer is 75.
If you then subtract 12 from 75 you get back to 63.
You can see this from the **number line**.

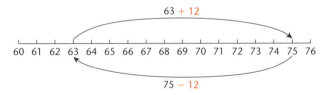

The order in which you add numbers does not matter:
$23 + 78 + 12$ is the same as $78 + 12 + 23$.

However the order does matter when you are subtracting:
$7 - 5$ is not the same as $5 - 7$.

When a calculation involves addition and subtraction you can
change the order to make it easier.
$12 - 15 + 6$ is the same as $12 + 6 - 15$.

You can use inverses to check additions and subtractions.
For example
$251 + 162 = 413$
Check:
$413 - 162 = 251$ ✓

If you change the order remember that each $+$ or $-$ sign applies to the number **after** it.

You can check using the inverse of subtraction or any other method. You must write down a reason why the answer is wrong.

Exam practice 1A

1 a Jane wrote $354 - 216 = 142$.
    Without working out the subtraction explain why Jane is wrong.
  b Pete wrote $276 - 77 = 199$.
    Is Pete correct? Give a reason for your answer.
  c Sally wrote $254 + 234 = 488$.
    Is Sally correct? Give a reason for your answer.
  d Jack wrote $172 + 352 = 524$.
    Is Jack correct? Give a reason for your answer.

2 There are 301 students in Year 7, 273 in Year 8 and 269 in Year 9.
   How many students are there altogether in Years 7, 8 and 9?

You can add numbers by writing them in a column. Make sure that the units, tens and hundreds are lined up.

3 At the end of last season a football club had 3459 members.
   This year they had 774 new members and 953 members left.
   How many members do they have now?

4 Work out:
   a 213 − 307 + 198 − 31
   b 29 + 108 − 210 + 93
   c 952 − 1010 − 251 + 438

Rearrange as
213 + 198 − 307 − 31

5 A book wholesaler had 493 copies of *Maths is Easy* in stock.
   They bought another 500 copies and sold 650 copies.
   How many did they have in stock after these transactions?

6 Find the missing numbers:
   a 278 + ☐ = 411   b 216 − ☐ = 125
   c 87 + ☐ = 225   d 632 − ☐ = 338
   e 342 − ☐ = 177   f 152 + ☐ = 395
   g 64 − 47 + ☐ = 234   h 133 + 63 − ☐ = 99
   i 44 − ☐ + 73 = 61

Class discussion
These calculations are wrong.
What is the mistake?
• 15 − 3 + 7 = 5
• 23 − 8 + 7 = 8

How can you make these calculations easy to do in your head?
• 2 + 7 + 8 + 3
• 27 − 18
• 128 + 19

7 Find the sum of one thousand and fifty, four hundred and seven,
   and three thousand five hundred.

8 Mont Blanc is 4810 m high and is the highest mountain in
   Europe.
   Mount Everest is 8843 m high.
   How much higher is Mount Everest than Mont Blanc?

9 Roger needs a total score of 301 to win a game of darts.
   On his first turn he scores 55. On his second turn he scores 87.
   How many does he still have to score to win?

10 A hall with four levels has 487 seats.
    For a concert the number of seats sold were: 104 for Level 1,
    87 for Level 2, 69 for Level 3 and 73 for Level 4.
    How many seats were not sold?

Mini coursework task
A number that reads the same forwards and backwards is called a
palindrome.
14241 and 636 are both palindromes.

Jenny says
   'If you take *any* number, reverse the digits and add the numbers
   together, then do the same with the result, and so on, you will end up
   with a palindrome.'
Investigate Jenny's statement. Do you think she is correct?

Starting with 352,
352 + 253 = 605
605 + 506 = 1111
which is a palindrome.

1.2 Multiplication and division

Multiplication and division are the inverse of each other.
If you multiply 12 by 8 the answer is 96:
If you divide 96 by 8 you get back to 12.

> You can use inverses to check multiplications and divisions.
> $183 \times 4 = 732$
> Check:
> $732 \div 4 = 183$ ✓

The order in which you multiply numbers does not matter:
    $4 \times 9 \times 6$ is the same as $6 \times 9 \times 4$.
However the order does matter when you are dividing:
    $12 \div 3$ is not the same as $3 \div 12$.

When a calculation involves multiplication and division you can change the order and do the division first:
    $12 \times 15 \div 6$ is the same as $12 \div 6 \times 15$.

> If you change the order remember that the operation ($\times$ or $\div$) applies to the number after it.

Exam practice 1B

1 Find:
   a 76×4 b 221×9 c 204×8
   d 132×7 e 953×3 f 211×4

> You can write numbers in a column to multiply:
> $$\begin{array}{r} 146 \\ \times \quad 6 \\ \hline 876 \\ \scriptstyle 2\,3 \end{array}$$

2 Find:
   a $85 \div 5$ b $152 \div 4$ c $306 \div 6$
   d $243 \div 9$ e $259 \div 7$ f $984 \div 8$

> You can divide the hundreds first, then the tens, then the units:
> $$\begin{array}{r} 3\;8 \\ 7\overline{)26\,{}^5 6} \end{array}$$

3 The pattern of numbers 3, 21, 147, ... is formed by multiplying the previous number by 7.
   Write down the next two numbers in the pattern.

4 Write down the missing digit in each calculation:
   a $3\square \times 4 = 136$ b $21 \times \square = 126$ c $\square 8 \times 8 = 384$

5 Find:
   a 36×10 b 51×100 c 108×1000
   d 560×100 e 30×46 f 72×200
   g 767×400 h 2000×233 i 6000×710

> You can multiply by 30 in two stages: multiply by 3 and then multiply the result by 10.
> So 45×30
> $= 45 \times 3 \times 10$
> $= 135 \times 10 = 1350$

1.3 Rounding numbers to the nearest 10, 100, 1000, ...

> To avoid mistakes you can draw a line after the digit in the place value you are rounding to.
> $8|3 = 80$ to the nearest ten.
> $29|6 = 300$ to the nearest ten.
> $5|78 = 600$ to the nearest hundred.
> $84|23 = 8400$ to the nearest hundred and
> $8|423 = 8000$ to the nearest thousand.

To round a number to a given place value, look at the next **digit**. If it is 5 or more, round up. If it is less than 5, round down.

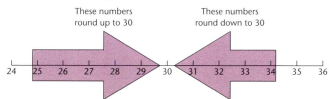

These numbers round up to 30   These numbers round down to 30

Estimating

You can **estimate** the answer to a calculation by **rounding** the numbers first.

An estimate is sometimes called an **approximation**.

You can use an estimate to check if an answer is the right sort of size.

> Rounding is like approximating but using a particular rule.

Example 1

Estimate 783×211 by rounding both numbers to the nearest hundred.

$$783 \times 211 \approx 800 \times 200$$
$$= 800 \times 2 \times 100$$
$$= 160\,000$$

> $\approx$ means 'is approximately equal to'.

Example 2

Find $278 - 122$.

Estimate: $300 - 100 = 200$

$278 - 122 = 156$

Compare with estimate: $156 \approx 200$ ✓

Exam practice 1C

1   Round each number to the nearest ten to find an approximate answer:
   a $95 - 39$ b $153 + 181$
   c $76 - 31 - 29$ d $295 + 304 - 451$

2   Four possible answers are given for each calculation. Three of them are wrong and one is correct.
   Without working them out, write down the letter of the correct answer.
   a $252 - 32$:   **A** 20   **B** 282   **C** 220   **D** 120
   b $748 + 412$:   **A** 338   **B** 1160   **C** 2550   **D** 960
   c $683 + 798 - 57$:   **A** 2784   **B** 424   **C** 1424   **D** 882
   d $56 - 188 + 421$:   **A** 665   **B** 289   **C** 177   **D** 433

3   Theresa wrote $737 - 76 = 761$. Theresa's answer is wrong.
   Without working out the subtraction, explain why Theresa's answer is wrong.

> If you subtract 76 from 737 is the answer bigger or smaller than 737?

A01 4 The answer given for each calculation is wrong.
Without working them out, explain why.
  a 856 + 248 = 848
  b 674 − 355 + 467 = 666
  c 145 + 487 − 223 = 576
  d 831 − 355 − 467 = 337

A01 5 Pat bought 6 printers priced at £129 each.
She was told the total cost was £650. This is not correct.
Without working out 129 × 6, decide if the total cost is more or less than £650. Explain how you decided.

A01 6 Three possible answers are given for each calculation.
Which of them are obviously wrong?
  a 253 × 2000 **A** 50 600   **B** 506 000   **C** 5 060 000
  b 521 × 36   **A** 1876   **B** 11 886   **C** 18 756
  c 400 × 250   **A** 100 000 **B** 25 000   **C** 10 000

A01 7 Three possible answers are given for each calculation.
Two of them are wrong and one is correct. Write down the letter of the correct answer.
  a 62 × 95   **A** 5890   **B** 6985   **C** 10 000
  b 88 × 27   **A** 2760   **B** 276   **C** 2376

A01 8 Envelopes are sold in packs of 50. Debby was asked how many envelopes there were in 400 of these packs,
She said
  '5 times 4 is twenty, then add two noughts for 400.
  There are 2000 envelopes in total.'
What is wrong with her reasoning?

1.4 Using a calculator

When you use a calculator you should always estimate your answer first. This will help tell you if you have made a mistake entering your calculation.

Exam practice 1D

1 Find:
  a 258 × 97   b 78 × 91   c 625 × 14
  d 89 × 484   e 2501 × 12

2 One jar of marmalade weighs 454 grams.
Find the weight of 124 jars.

3 A car park has 34 rows and each row has 42 parking spaces. How many cars can be parked?

Class discussion

Each of these questions contains numbers. To answer the questions you will need to add, subtract, multiply or divide these numbers. What are the clues that tell you what to do?

1 At the end of last season a football club had 8459 members. This year 974 members joined and 753 members left. How many members do they have now?

2 The counter on Gina's car showed a total mileage of 32743 at the end of Wednesday. Gina did 143 miles on Monday, 55 miles on Tuesday and 83 miles on Wednesday. What was the reading when she set out on Monday morning?

3 There are 667 seats in the school hall. They are arranged in 23 rows with the same number of seats in each row. How many seats are there in a row?

4 A lorry is loaded with identical boxes. The total weight of the boxes is 1404 kg. One box weighs 18 kg. How many boxes are there?

Estimate your answer first.

4   A shop takes delivery of 48 crates of bottled water.
Each crate contains 48 bottles.
How many bottles are delivered?

5   A college wants to transport 752 students to the theatre in buses.
Each bus can take 47 students.
How many buses are needed?

6   A light bulb was tested by being left on continuously.
It worked for exactly 48 days.
For how many hours was it working?

7   Find the missing digits in these calculations.

a $3\square \times 32 = 992$ b $215 \times \square 6 = 3440$

c $354 \times 3\square = 12\,390$ d $768 \div 32 = 2\square$

e $945 \div 35 = 2\square$ f $858 \div 3\square = 26$

1.5 Remainders

When you multiply two whole numbers together, the result is always a whole number. When a whole number is divided by another whole number you sometimes get a remainder.

When you answer problems that involve remainders, you may need to round the answer.
Read the question carefully to decide whether you need to round up or down.

$12 \div 5$ means 'How many fives are there in twelve?'
There are 2 fives in twelve with 2 units left over. These 2 units are called the remainder. This is written as
$12 \div 5 = 2$ remainder 2.

Example 3

June has 50 loose eggs and some egg boxes.
One egg box holds 12 eggs.
a   How many egg boxes can June fill?
b   How many egg boxes does June need to pack all the eggs?

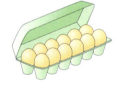

a $50 \div 12 = 4$, remainder 2

June can fill 4 boxes.

The two eggs left over will not fill a box.

b   She needs 5 egg boxes.

To put all the eggs into boxes, June needs another box for the 2 eggs left over.

When numbers are simple you can work in your head.

Exam practice 1E

1   Work in your head and just write down the remainder for each calculation:

a $39 \div 8$ b $80 \div 9$ c $55 \div 3$ d $130 \div 12$

2   Eggs are packed into boxes that each hold six eggs.
How many boxes are needed to pack 730 eggs?

3   A group of 150 people is going to the theatre.
    A coach will seat 35 people.
    a   How many coaches are needed?
    b   How many spare seats will there be?

4   Nine teachers are taking 134 Year 9 students and 89 Year 10
    students on a trip.
    How many minibuses should they order if each minibus can
    carry 19 people?

5   A male voice choir of 85 singers was going on tour.
    To get to the airport they chartered 15-seater minibuses.
    a   How many did they need?
    b   Were there any spare seats? If so, how many?

6   An allotment is 1000 cm long.
    Lettuces are planted 30 cm apart in rows down the length of the
    plot.
    The first lettuce is 5 cm from the end of the row.
    How many lettuces can be planted in one row?

1.6 Mixed calculations

When there are brackets in a calculation, work out the part inside the
bracket first.

Example 4

Work out $4 \times (2 + 5)$.

$4 \times (2 + 5) = 4 \times 7$
$ = 28$

> Work out $2 + 5$ first.

When a calculation contains a mixture of operations do
multiplication and division before addition and subtraction.

Example 5

Work out: a $2 \times 4 + 3 \times 6$ b $4 - 14 \div 7 + 3$.

a $2 \times 4 + 3 \times 6 = 8 + 18$
$ = 26$

> Do the multiplications first.

b $4 - 14 \div 7 + 3 = 4 - 2 + 3$
$ = 5$

> Do the division first.

The correct order of operations is:
        Brackets first, then division and multiplication,
                then addition and subtraction.

Exam practice 1F

1 Work out:
   a $2 + 4 \times 6 - 8$
   b $7 + (4 - 3) \times 2$
   c $5 \times 3 \times 4 \div 12 + 6 - 2$
   d $24 \div 8 - 3$
   e $7 \times (2 + 6) - 1$
   f $9 \div 3 - 2 + 1 + 6 \times 2$

> You can do these in your head.

2 Calculate:
   a $(7 + 3) \times 2 - 8 \times 2$
   b $8 + 3 \times 2 - 4 \div 2$
   c $6 + 8 \div 4 + 6 \times 3 \div 2$
   d $20 \div (9 - 4) + 3$
   e $(7 + 30) \times 2 - 45$
   f $25 \times (4 + 6) \div 2$

3 A youth club started the year with 82 members.
   During the year 58 people joined and 94 people left.
   How many members were there at the end of the year ?

4 One bar of chocolate costs 45p. Shona bought 3 of these bars.
   She paid with a £5 note. How much change did she get?

5 Each part of this ladder is 200 cm long.
   There is an overlap of 20 cm at each junction.
   How long is the extended ladder?

6 In a mathematics book the answers start on page 126 and end on
   page 134.
   How many pages of answers are there?

7 My great-grandfather died in 1945, aged 72. In which year was
   he born?

> There are two possible answers to question 7 and to question 8.

8 A cedar tree was planted in the year in which Lord Toff was born.
   He died in 1980, aged 90.
   a In what year was Lord Toff born?
   b How old was the tree in 2005?

9 A second-hand car dealer had 36 cars in stock on 1st March.
   In March and April he sold 65 cars and took delivery of 84.
   How many cars were in stock at the end of April?

1.7 Negative numbers

Negative numbers are written with a minus sign in front.
For example, you write negative 2 as -2.

Numbers greater than zero are called **positive numbers**.

Positive and negative numbers together are known as
directed numbers.
Directed numbers can be fractions or decimals.

Integers are the numbers ... $-3, -2, -1, 0, 1, 2, 3, ...$

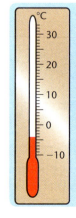

> A temperature of 2°C below freezing is marked as -2 on the scale.
> This thermometer shows a reading of -4. It is 4°C below 0°.
> 0°C is the freezing point of water.

A line marked with positive and negative numbers is called a number line.

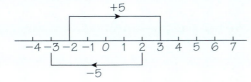

On this number line:

5 is to the right of 3 so $5 > 3$

2 is to the left of 6 so $2 < 6$

> $>$ means 'is greater than'
> $<$ means 'is less than'.

Addition and subtraction

To add a positive number, move right along the number line.

To subtract a positive number, move left along the number line.

Example 6

Find: **a** $-2 + 5$ **b** $2 - 5$.

> 2 is a positive number. You can write 2 as $+2$, but the $+$ is usually left out.

a $-2 + 5 = 3$ **b** $2 - 5 = -3$

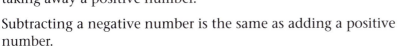

Adding a negative number is the same as subtracting a positive number.

To freeze water you have to reduce its temperature. You can think of this either as adding coldness (negative heat) or as taking away warmth (positive heat), so adding a negative number is the same as taking away a positive number.

Subtracting a negative number is the same as adding a positive number.

An ice cube starts at $-6°C$. To melt it you have to take away $-6°C$. So you have to increase its temperature by $6°C$, giving $-(-6°C) = +6°C$.

Example 7

Find: **a** $1 + (-4)$ **b** $2 - (-5)$.

> Putting brackets round the negative number makes it easier to read.

a $1 + (-4) = 1 - 4$
            $= -3$

> Adding -4 is the same as subtracting 4.

b $2 - (-5) = 2 + 5$
            $= 7$

> Subtracting -5 is the same as adding 5.

Exam practice 1G

1 Place these numbers in order of size with the smallest first.
   a $1, -2, -4$
   b $-5, -2, -4$
   c $3, -2, 7, -3$
   d $5, -5, 3, -3$

2 a Place these numbers in order of size with the smallest first.
      $-1, 0, -3, 1, -5, -9$
   b Place these numbers in order of size with the largest first.
      $6, -4, -6, 4, 0, -2$

3 Find: a $4 - 7$
          b $-2 + 6$
          c $3 + (-5)$
          d $-6 + 9$
          e $-4 - (-2)$
          f $8 - (-5)$
          g $12 + (-8)$
          h $-12 - (-8)$
          i $-12 - 8$

You can work these in your head.

4 Find the missing numbers:
   a $7 - 9 = \square$
   b $4 - \square = -2$
   c $3 - 5 = \square$
   d $\square + 4 = -6$
   e $\square - 5 = -3$
   f $8 - \square = 10$

You can use a number line to help.

5 Find:
   a $7 - 9 + 4$
   b $10 - 4 - 9$
   c $-2 - 3 + 9$
   d $-3 - 4 + 2$
   e $-4 + 2 + 5$
   f $-5 + 6 - 7$
   g $-2 - (-5) - 1$
   h $3 + (-3) - (-2)$
   i $-18 - (-20)$

6 When Keri boarded a plane in the Caribbean the temperature was 26°C.
   On the plane the temperature outside the aircraft was -57°C.
   What was the difference between these two temperatures?

Difference means (larger number) − (smaller number).

7 The time in Hong Kong is 7 hours ahead of the time in Rome.
   a What time is it in Rome when it is 8 a.m. in Hong Kong?
   b What time is it in Hong Kong when it is 8 a.m. in Rome?

This means the time in Hong Kong is Rome time + 7 hours.

8 The time in Perth, Australia, is London time plus 8 hours.
   Lorna works in London.
   She arranges to phone a colleague at 5 p.m. Perth time. What time in London should she ring?

9 A pendulum is held with the string at an angle of 28° to the vertical and released.
   It swings through an arc of 45°, back 43°, forward 42°, back 40°, forward 38° and back 37° before being held still.
   What is the final angle the string makes with the vertical?

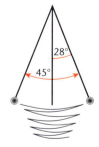

10 The time in Athens is UK time + 2 hours.
    The time in Florida is UK time − 6 hours.
    a When it is 6 p.m. in the UK, what time is it in
       i Athens
       ii Florida?
    b Kathy catches a plane in Florida at 11 a.m. local time and flies direct to Athens. The journey takes 9 hours.
       What is the local time in Athens when Kathy arrives?

Mini coursework task

The numbers in this triangular pattern are formed by finding the difference between the two numbers in the row above.

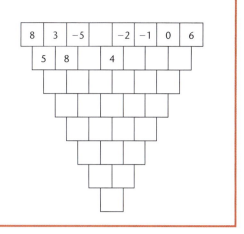

Copy the diagram and fill in the empty spaces.
Is there more than one way in which the triangle can be completed?

1.8 Multiplication and division of directed numbers

When two numbers are multiplied or divided
if the signs are the same (both + or both −), the result is positive,
if the signs are different (one + and one −), the result is negative.

Example 8

Work out: **a** -8×6 **b** $(2 - 5) \div (-3)$.

a $-8 \times 6 = -48$ The signs are different so the answer is negative.

b $(2 - 5) \div (-3) = -3 \div (-3)$ Find $2 - 5$ first.

$\qquad\qquad = 1$

The signs are the same, so the answer is positive.

Exam practice 1H

1 Work out:

  a $4 + 3 \times (-4)$ **b** $8 + 2 \div (-2)$

  c $(-2) \times 3 + 4 \times (-5)$ **d** $2 - 4 \times (-2)$

  e $12 + 3 \times (-6)$ **f** $(5 - 8) \div (2 - 5)$

  g $-4 \div (-2)$ **h** $(2 - 10) \div (-4 \times 2)$

  i $(3 - 5) \div (-2)$ **j** $2 \times (-2) \times (-3)$

  k $(-2) \times 3 - 10 \div (-2)$ **l** $5 - 2 \div (-1)$

  m $(-4) \times (-5)$ **n** $(-1) \times (-2) \times 2$

  p $-3 \times (-5) \times (-2) + 7$

Remember: brackets first, then multiplication and division, then addition and subtraction.

2 a Find a number that when multiplied by itself equals 25.
  b Find a different number with the same property.

3 a What number has to be multiplied by − 6 to get 42?
  b What number must you divide − 20 by to get 5?
  c What number has to be multiplied by − 8 to get − 32?
  d What number must you divide − 18 by to get − 6?

4 Look at this pattern of numbers: − 3, 9, − 27, 81, − 243
   What do you multiply each number by to get the next one?

5 Look at this pattern of numbers: − 4, 8, − 16, 32, − 64
  a What do you multiply each number by to get the next one?
  b Write down the next two numbers in the pattern.

6 Insert = and one of the symbols +, −, ×, ÷ to produce a correct
   calculation. Keep the numbers in the order given.

> You can put brackets
> around a directed
> number.

  a 4 ☐ 1 ☐ − 3   b 2 ☐ 3 ☐ 5   c 6 ☐ − 2 ☐ − 3
  d 5 ☐ − 2 ☐ 7   e 2 ☐ − 4 ☐ − 2   f 5 ☐ − 4 ☐ 9

7 Frank sat an examination with 10 questions.
   For each question, five possible answers were given and Frank
   had to tick the answer he thought was correct.
   For each answer he got correct he scored 2 points.
   For each answer he got wrong he lost a point.
   If he failed to attempt a question he scored nothing.
  a What was his highest possible score?
  b What was his lowest possible score?
  c Frank got 6 questions correct, 2 wrong and he did not
     attempt the rest.
     What did Frank score in the examination?

8 Pete bought a car for £12 000.
   Each year for the next 8 years it went down in value by £1400.
   By this time it had become collectable.
   For the next 3 years its value went up by £1000 a year.
   What was it worth at the end of this time?

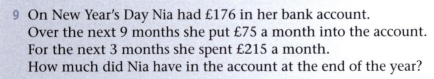

9 On New Year's Day Nia had £176 in her bank account.
   Over the next 9 months she put £75 a month into the account.
   For the next 3 months she spent £215 a month.
   How much did Nia have in the account at the end of the year?

10 Find the value of $5 - x$ when
  a $x = -2$ b $x = 7$.

> Replace x by − 2
> so $5 - x$ becomes
> $5 - (-2)$.

11 Find the value of $y - x$ when
  a $y = 3$ and $x = 7$ b $y = -4$ and $x = 3$
  c $y = -3$ and $x = -7$.

12 Find the value of $4 - t - 2 \times s$ when
  a $t = 3$ and $s = 5$ b $t = 3$ and $s = -5$
  c $t = -3$ and $s = -5$.

Summary of key points

- The order in which you add or multiply numbers does not matter.
- The order in which you subtract or divide numbers is important.
- You can round a number to a given place value by looking at the next digit. If it is 5 or more, round up. If it is less than 5 round down.
- The order of operations is brackets first, then multiplication and division, then addition and subtraction.
- Adding a negative number is the same as subtracting a positive number.
- Subtracting a negative number is the same as adding a positive number.
- If two numbers are multiplied or divided, then
    if the signs are the same (both + or both −), the result is positive
    if the signs are different (one + and one −), the result is negative.

Most students who get GRADE C or above can:
- work with directed numbers,
- estimate answers to calculations with whole numbers.

Glossary

Approximation	a rough value
Counting numbers	the numbers 1, 2, 3, 4, …
Difference	(larger number) − (smaller number)
Digit	one of the symbols 0, 1, 2, …, 8, 9
Directed numbers	positive and negative numbers together are called directed numbers
Estimate	a rough value, the same as approximate
Integers	the numbers …− 2, − 1, 0, 1, 2, …
Natural numbers	the numbers 1, 2, 3, 4, …
Negative number	a number below zero, e.g. negative 3, written as − 3
Number line	a line marked with numbers going in both directions:

$$-6 \quad -5 \quad -4 \quad -3 \quad -2 \quad -1 \quad 0 \quad 1 \quad 2 \quad 3 \quad 4 \quad 5 \quad 6$$

Palindrome	a number that reads the same forwards and backwards
Positive number	a number greater than zero
Rounding	writing a number correct to a given place value
Whole numbers	the numbers 0, 1, 2, 3, … (the natural numbers plus zero)

2 Factors, primes and indices

This chapter will show you:	Before you start you need to know:
✓ what a prime number is ✓ how to use indices to write a number as the product of prime factors ✓ how to find the highest common factor and the least common multiple of a set of numbers ✓ how to solve problems using highest common factors and least common multiples ✓ how to find the square roots and cube root of a number	✓ your multiplication tables up to 10×10 ✓ how to divide by whole numbers less than 10

2.1 Factors and primes

A **factor** of a number divides into the number exactly leaving no remainder.

> The factors of 12 are 1, 2, 3, 4, 6 and 12.

The following tests for dividing by different numbers are useful:
- an even number will divide by 2
- a number whose digits add up to a multiple of 3 will divide by 3
- a number ending in 5 or 0 will divide by 5
- a number whose digits add up to a multiple of 9 will divide by 9.

> **Did you know that**
> - 2 is the only even prime number
> - prime numbers often occur as consecutive odd numbers such as 29 and 31
> - there is no pattern to get the next prime number from one you know
> - there are infinitely many prime numbers?

A **prime number** has only two factors: 1 and itself.

Note that 1 is not a prime number since it has only one factor.

> 5 is a prime number, as the only factors of 5 are 1 and 5.

Exam practice 2A

1. Express each number as the product of two factors in as many ways as you can.

   a 18   b 36   c 48   d 60   e 45   f 144

   > $18 = 2 \times 9$. There are two other ways of writing 18 as the product of two factors.

A01
2. a John said that 747 and 429 are exactly divisible by 3. Is John correct? Give a reason for your answer.

   b Colin said that 207 and 5675 are exactly divisible by 9. Is Colin correct? Give a reason for your answer.

3 Which of these numbers is exactly divisible by 3?
   a 357   b 3896   c 88 551   d 56 725   e 33 447

4 Which of these numbers is exactly divisible by 9?
   a 369   b 3897   c 88 569   d 56 725   e 33 444

5 Which of the following are prime numbers?
   16, 29, 41, 42, 57, 91, 101, 127

A01 6 Sandy said that 8820 is divisible by 15.
   a Explain why Sandy is correct.
   b He then said that 8820 is divisible by 80.
      Is he still correct? Give a reason for your answer.

> If a number is divisible by 3 and 5 it is divisible by 15.

7 a Is 21 168 divisible by 6?   b Is 30 870 divisible by 15?

8 a Write each even number from 8 to 20 as the sum of two odd prime numbers.
   b Write each odd number between 10 and 30 as the sum of three odd prime numbers.

A01 9 Write 'true' or 'false' for each of the following statements.
   Give reasons for your answers.
   a All the prime numbers are odd numbers.
   b All odd numbers are prime numbers.
   c All prime numbers between 10 and 100 are odd numbers.
   d The only even prime number is 2.
   e There are six prime numbers less than 10.
   f The largest prime number less than 100 is 91.

> You can use an example to show that a statement is not true.
> 'The sum of two odd numbers is odd' is not true because $1 + 3 = 4$ which is even. This is called a **counter example**.

A01 10 The prime numbers 3 and 47 add up to 50.
   Ken said that there are other pairs of prime numbers that add up to 50?
   Is Ken correct? Give a reason for your answer.

Mini coursework task

A number is abundant if the sum of its factors is more than twice the number itself.
a Show that 12 and 18 are abundant numbers.
b Find two more abundant numbers.
c 'Any multiple of an abundant number is abundant.'
   Investigate this statement. Do you think it is true?

> 8 is not an abundant number. The sum of its factors is $1 + 2 + 4 + 8 = 15$ which is less than $8 \times 2 = 16$.

2.2 Index notation

The expression 2^4 is an example of index notation.

This is the **index** or **power**.

$2^4 = 2 \times 2 \times 2 \times 2$

This is the **base**.

> $7^3 = 7 \times 7 \times 7$. The base is 7 and the index is 3.

You say 'two to the power 4' or 'two to the four'.

Example 1

Write each of the following in index form.

a $6 \times 6 \times 6$
b $9 \times 9 \times 9 \times 8 \times 8$

a $6 \times 6 \times 6 = 6^3$

6^3 is called 'six cubed'.

b $9 \times 9 \times 9 \times 8 \times 8 = 9^3 \times 8^2$

Exam practice 2B

1 Write each of the following in index form.
  a $2 \times 2 \times 2$
  b $3 \times 3 \times 3$
  c $7 \times 7 \times 7 \times 7$
  d $5 \times 5 \times 5 \times 5 \times 5$

A01

2 **a** Paula said that $3 \times 3 \times 3 \times 3 \times 3 \times 3$ is 3^5.
    Is Paula correct? Give a reason for your answer.
  b James wrote $6 \times 6 \times 6 \times 6 = 6^4$.
    Is James correct? Give a reason for your answer.

3 Find the value of **a** 3^3 **b** 5^2 **c** 2^5 **d** 3^4.

5^2 is called 'five squared'.

A01

4 **a** Zoe said the value of 3^3 was 9.
    Is Zoe correct? Give a reason for your answer.
  b Bill said the value of 2^4 was 16.
    Is Bill correct? Give a reason for your answer.

5 Write down the squares of each of the numbers from 1 to 15.

6 Write down the cubes of each of the numbers from 1 to 15.

The cube of 7 is $7^3 = 7 \times 7 \times 7 = 343$.

7 Express each of the following in index form:
  a $2 \times 2 \times 5 \times 5$
  b $3 \times 3 \times 3 \times 2 \times 2$
  c $2 \times 3 \times 3 \times 5 \times 2 \times 5$
  d $7 \times 7 \times 7 \times 3 \times 5 \times 7 \times 3$
  e $17 \times 5 \times 17 \times 5 \times 17$

A01

8 Di said that $3 \times 5 \times 5 \times 3 \times 7 \times 3 \times 7$ in index form is $3^3 \times 5^3 \times 7^2$.
  Is Di correct? Give a reason for your answer.

9 Find the value of
  a $2^2 \times 3^3$
  b $3^2 \times 5^2$
  c $2^2 \times 3^2 \times 5$
  d $2 \times 3^2 \times 7$.

10 Express these numbers as powers of prime numbers.
  a 4   **b** 8   **c** 49   **d** 32
  e 9   **f** 64   **g** 625   **h** 16 807

Find a prime number that divides exactly into the number, then keep on dividing by it.

2.3 Expressing a number as the product of prime factors

When a factor of a number is prime it is called a **prime factor**.

You can write any number that is not a prime as a product of prime factors.

This is known as the Fundamental Theorem of Arithmetic.

When a number is small you can do this by breaking the factors down in stages.

Example 2

Express 48 as a product of its prime factors.

$48 = 4 \times 12$
$\quad = 2 \times 2 \times 3 \times 4$
$\quad = 2 \times 2 \times 3 \times 2 \times 2 = 2^4 \times 3$

Start by writing 48 as the product of any two factors: $48 = 4 \times 12$.
Then each factor that is not prime can be written as the product of two factors. You can repeat this until all the factors are prime numbers.

A more organised approach helps for larger numbers.

Example 3

Express 2100 as a product of its prime factors.

$2100 \div 2 = 1050$
$1050 \div 2 = 525$
$\ 525 \div 3 = 175$
$\ 175 \div 5 = 35$
$\ \ \ 35 \div 5 = 7$
$\ \ \ \ \ 7 \div 7 = 1$

So $2100 = 2 \times 2 \times 3 \times 5 \times 5 \times 7$
$\qquad\quad = 2^2 \times 3 \times 5^2 \times 7$

Start by dividing by 2 as many times as possible.
Then divide by 3 as many times as possible. Then divide by each prime number in turn until you are left with 1.

Highest common factor

Two or more numbers can have the same factor. This is called a common factor.

7 is a common factor of 14, 28 and 42.

The **highest common factor** of two or more numbers is the largest number that divides exactly into all of them.

Highest common factor is sometimes written as HCF.

You can find the HCF by writing each number as a product of prime factors.

Example 4

Find the highest common factor of:

a   108 and 204   **b**   14, 28 and 42   **c**   148 and 152.

a $108 = \underline{2} \times \underline{2} \times \underline{3} \times 3 \times 3$ and $204 = \underline{2} \times \underline{2} \times \underline{3} \times 17$

So $2 \times 2 \times 3 = 12$ is the HCF of 108 and 204.

> The HCF is the product of the prime factors that are common to 108 and 204.

b $14 = \underline{2} \times \underline{7}$, $28 = \underline{2} \times 2 \times \underline{7}$, $42 = \underline{2} \times 3 \times \underline{7}$

So $2 \times 7 = 14$ is the HCF of 14, 28 and 42.

c $148 = \underline{2} \times \underline{2} \times 37$, $152 = \underline{2} \times \underline{2} \times 2 \times 19$

The HCF is $2 \times 2 = 4$.

> The HCF is the product of the prime factors that are common to 148 and 152.

Exam practice 2C

1. Find the largest whole number that will divide exactly into
   a   9 and 12   **b**   8 and 16   **c**   12 and 24
   d   25, 50 and 75   **e**   22, 33 and 44   **f**   21, 42 and 84.

2. Find the largest whole number that will divide exactly into
   a   39, 13 and 26   **b**   12, 18, 20 and 36.

3. **a**   Mandy said that the largest whole number that will divide exactly into 14 and 42 is 7.
   Is Mandy correct? Give a reason for your answer.
   b   George said that 8 is the largest whole number that will divide exactly into 36, 44, 52 and 56.
   Is George correct? Give a reason for your answer.

4. Find the HCF of
   a   90 and 65   **b**   18 and 54   **c**   20 and 24
   d   504 and 396   **e**   54 and 36   **f**   171, 126 and 81.

5. This rectangular floor is to be covered with square tiles.
   What is the side length of the largest tile that can be used to cover the floor exactly?

   350 cm

   450 cm

   > The side of the square has to divide exactly into 350 and 450.

6. Harry has a rectangular piece of chipboard measuring 42 cm by 30 cm.
   He wants to divide it into equal squares.
   What is the largest possible square Harry can use?

7. Work out the largest number of students who can share equally 105 apples and 63 oranges.

8. Three metal rods with lengths 182 cm, 273 cm and 294 cm are sawn into equal-sized pieces.
   Work out the greatest possible length for these pieces if there is no waste.

2.4 Multiples

When a number is multiplied by a whole number the result is a **multiple** of the first number.

3, 6, 9, 12, 15, … are all multiples of 3. $300 = 100 \times 3$ and $153 = 51 \times 3$ are also multiples of 3.

Least common multiple

One number can be a multiple of two or more numbers. This is called a common multiple.

The **least common multiple** of two or more numbers is the smallest number that all of them will divide into exactly.

You can find the LCM of small numbers by writing down some multiples of each number.

Least common multiple is sometimes written as LCM.

Example 5

Find the LCM of 6, 8 and 10.

Multiples of 10: 10, 20, 30, 40, 50, 60, 70, 80, 90, 100, 110, **120**, ….
Multiples of 6: 30, 60, 90, **120**, 180, 210, 240, …
Multiples of 8: 40, 80, **120**, …

The LCM of 6, 8 and 10 is 120.

Multiples of ten end in zero, so you only need to list multiples of 6 and 8 that end in zero.

It helps to write larger numbers as a product of prime factors.

Example 6

Find the LCM of **a** 48 and 52   **b** 108 and 204.

a $48 = 2 \times 2 \times 2 \times 2 \times 3$
$52 = 2 \times 2 \times 13$
The LCM is $2 \times 2 \times 2 \times 2 \times 3 \times 13 = 624$.

b $108 = 2^2 \times 3^3$
$204 = 2^2 \times 3 \times 17$
LCM is $2^2 \times 3^3 \times 17 = 1836$.

Express each number as a product of prime factors.
To find the LCM, start with the prime factors of the smaller number then put in those factors of the larger number that are not already included.

Exam practice 2D

1 Find the least common multiple of
   a 2 and 3   **b** 6 and 15   **c** 18 and 24   **d** 12 and 15.

2 Find the LCM of
   a 9, 12 and 18   **b** 12, 16 and 24
   c 3, 8 and 12   **d** 24, 30 and 36.

3 a Andy said that the least common multiple of 15 and 18 is 90.
     Is Andy correct? Give a reason for your answer.

  b Hetty said that the least common multiple of 24 and 36 is 144.
     Is Hetty correct? Give a reason for your answer.

4 Two model trains travel round a double track.
  One train completes the circuit in 12 seconds and
  the other completes the circuit in 15 seconds.
  If they start side by side how long will it be before
  they are side by side again?

12 s and 15 s
both need to
divide exactly
into the time.

5 Rectangular tiles measure 15 cm by 9 cm.
  What is the length of the side of the smallest square area that can
  be exactly covered with these tiles?

6 Steve, Sally and Darren all go to Mrs James for music lessons.
  Steve goes every fourth day, Sally every eighth day and Darren
  every sixth day.
  They all go for a lesson on Monday, 1st February.
  On what date and day of the week will they next all have a lesson
  on the same day?

7 Three bells ring at intervals of 8 seconds, 12 seconds and
  15 seconds. All three bells ring together.
  How many seconds will it be before they ring together again?

8 The church at Bracksford has a peel of four bells.
       No.1 bell rings every 5 seconds,
       No.2 bell rings every 6 seconds,
       No.3 bell rings every 7 seconds,
       No.4 bell rings every 8 seconds.
  All four bells ring together.
  How long will it be before they ring together again?

2.5 Roots

Square roots

When a number is the product of two equal factors, each factor is
called a square root of the number.
  $4 = 2 \times 2$, so 2 is a square root of 4.
  $4 = (-2) \times (-2)$, so -2 is also a square root of 4.

**Any positive number has two square roots, one positive and
one negative.**

$\sqrt{64}$ means the positive square root of 64, so $\sqrt{64} = 8$
and $-\sqrt{64}$ means the negative square root of 64, so $-\sqrt{64} = -8$.

A negative number
cannot have a
square root because
a negative number
cannot be expressed
as the product of
two equal factors.
You can only get a
negative number by
multiplying a negative
number and a positive
number.

A whole number whose square root is also a whole number is called a **perfect square**.

You can find the square root of a perfect square by expressing it as a product of its prime factors in index form.

Example 7

Find $\sqrt{784}$.

$784 = 2^4 \times 7^2$

$\sqrt{784} = 2^2 \times 7^1 = 4 \times 7 = 28$

> Halve each index.

Example 8

What is the smallest number you need to multiply by 28 to give a perfect square?

$28 = 2^2 \times 7$

$28 \times 7 = 2^2 \times 7^2$ which is a perfect square.

7 is the smallest number.

> Write 28 as a product of prime factors. For a perfect square all the indices must be even, so another 7 is needed.

Cube Roots

When a number is the product of three equal factors, each factor is called a cube root of the number.

$\sqrt[3]{8}$ means the cube root of 8, so $\sqrt[3]{8} = 2$.

Each number has only one cube root.
If the number is positive the cube root is positive. $\sqrt[3]{27} = 3$

If the number is negative the cube root is negative. $\sqrt[3]{-8} = -2$

> Check:
> $(-2) \times (-2) \times (-2)$
> $= 4 \times (-2) = -8$

Example 9

The number 9261 has an exact cube root. Find it without using a calculator.

$9261 = 3^3 \times 7^3$

$\sqrt[3]{9261} = 3^1 \times 7^1 = 3 \times 7 = 21$

> Write the number as a product of prime factors. Divide each power by 3 to give the cube root.

Exam practice 2E

1 Write down the square roots of **a** 16 **b** 25 **c** 81 **d** 169 **e** 144.

A01

2 Dave said that one of the square roots of 256 is -16.
   Is Dave correct? Give a reason for your answer.

> Remember that every positive number has two square roots, one positive and one negative.

3 Find the square roots of 400.

4 a Express 484 as a product of prime factors and hence find $\sqrt{484}$.
  b Express 324 as a product of prime factors and hence find its square roots.

5 One square root of 3136 is -56. Write down the other.

6 Find
  a $\sqrt{5625}$ b $\sqrt{1225}$ c $\sqrt{2704}$ d $\sqrt{38\,416}$ e $\sqrt{3600}$.

7 Write down the cube root of   a 125   b -8 c 1000.

8 Ed said that the cube root of -27 is 3.
  Is Ed correct? Give a reason for your answer.

9 What is $\sqrt[3]{1000}$?

10 Express each number as a product of prime factors in index form and hence find its cube root.
   a 512   b 3375   c 1728

11 Work out the cube root of -216.

12 Find the smallest integer you need to multiply by 24 to make a number that has an exact square root.

13 Find the smallest number you need to multiply by 40 to make a number that is a perfect square.

Summary of key points

- $2 \times 2 \times 2 \times 2 \times 2$ can be written as 2^5. The upper number is called the index or power. The lower number is called the base.
- A whole number can be expressed as the product of prime factors. For example, $504 = 2^3 \times 3^2 \times 7$.
- The highest common factor (HCF) of two or more numbers is the largest number that divides exactly into all of them. For example the HCF of 4, 6 and 8 is 2.
- The least common multiple (LCM) for two or more numbers is the smallest number that is a multiple of all of them. For example the LCM of 4, 6 and 8 is 24.
- Any positive number has two square roots, one positive and one negative. A negative number does not have a square root.
- A number has only one cube root. The cube root of a positive number is positive and the cube root of a negative number is negative.

Most students who get GRADE C or above can:

- write a number as a product of prime factors
- find the HCF and LCM of small numbers.

Glossary

Base	the number which is raised to a power, e.g. the base of 3^6 is 3
Counter example	an example used to show that a statement is not true
Factor	a whole number that will divide into a given whole number without leaving a remainder
Highest common factor	the highest whole number that will divide into two or more whole numbers without leaving a remainder
Index (plural indices)	another name for power which tells you how many of the base number to multiply together e.g. the index of 6^3 is 3
Least common multiple	the lowest whole number that two or more whole numbers will divide into without remainders e.g. the LCM of 12, 16 and 21 is 336
Multiple	a number that has the given number as a factor e.g. 12 is a multiple of 3 because 3 is a factor of 12
Perfect square	a whole number whose square root is a whole number
Power	the same as index
Prime factor	a factor of a number that is also a prime number
Prime number	a number that has exactly two factors: itself and 1

3 Fractions

This chapter will show you:
- ✓ how to find equivalent fractions
- ✓ how to order a set of fractions according to size
- ✓ how to convert between mixed numbers and improper fractions
- ✓ how to express one quantity as a fraction of another
- ✓ how to add, subtract, multiply and divide fractions
- ✓ how to find fractions of a quantity
- ✓ how to find the reciprocal of a fraction
- ✓ how to solve word problems using fractions

Before you start you need to know:
- ✓ how to add and subtract whole numbers
- ✓ how to divide by a whole number
- ✓ how to find the least common multiple of two or more numbers

3.1 Fractions

A **fraction** is part of a unit or quantity.

The fraction 'three-quarters' is written $\frac{3}{4}$.

This is the **numerator**.

This is the **denominator**.

Equivalent fractions

The fractions $\frac{4}{8}$, $\frac{3}{6}$, $\frac{2}{4}$, and $\frac{1}{2}$ are all the same size.

They are called **equivalent fractions**.

You can find equivalent fractions by multiplying (or dividing) the numerator and the denominator by the same number.

Dividing the numerator and denominator by the same number gives an equivalent fraction with a smaller numerator and denominator. This is called **simplifying the fraction** or **cancelling**.

When the fraction has been simplified to give the smallest possible numerator and denominator, it is in its **lowest possible terms**, or simplest form.

Did you know

that writing a fraction with one number above the other like $\frac{3}{4}$ was probably started by a Hindu named Brahmagupta? The line between the two numbers came later.

Example 1

a Write $\frac{1}{5}$ as an equivalent fraction with denominator 15.

b Write $\frac{15}{75}$ in its lowest possible terms.

a $\frac{1}{5} = \frac{3}{15}$ (×3)

b $\frac{15}{75} = \frac{\overset{1}{\cancel{15}}}{\underset{5}{\cancel{75}}} = \frac{1}{5}$

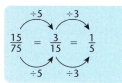

You need to write $\frac{1}{5}$ as $\frac{\square}{15}$.
$5 \times 3 = 15$, so multiply top and bottom by 3.

$\frac{15}{75} = \frac{3}{15} = \frac{1}{5}$ (÷5 ÷3)

Exam practice 3A

1 Express these fractions as eighths: **a** $\frac{1}{2}$ **b** $\frac{1}{4}$ **c** $\frac{3}{4}$

2 Express these fractions as twelfths: **a** $\frac{1}{2}$ **b** $\frac{2}{3}$ **c** $\frac{3}{4}$ **d** $\frac{1}{6}$

3 Write each of these fractions as equivalent fractions with denominator 45.

   a $\frac{2}{15}$ **b** $\frac{4}{9}$ **c** $\frac{14}{15}$ **d** $\frac{3}{5}$

4 Complete these fractions: $\frac{2}{5} = \frac{\square}{10} = \frac{6}{\square} = \frac{\square}{25}$

5 Express each of these fractions in its lowest terms.

   a $\frac{5}{60}$ **b** $\frac{27}{36}$ **c** $\frac{48}{84}$ **d** $\frac{99}{132}$

6 Simplify these fractions as much as possible.

   a $\frac{24}{60}$ **b** $\frac{36}{90}$ **c** $\frac{36}{72}$ **d** $\frac{27}{90}$

3.2 Comparing the sizes of fractions

To compare fractions with different denominators change them into equivalent fractions with the same denominator.

Example 2

Which is the smaller: $\frac{2}{9}$ or $\frac{1}{6}$?

$$\frac{2}{9} = \frac{4}{18}$$

and $\frac{1}{6} = \frac{3}{18}$

$\frac{3}{18} < \frac{4}{18}$ so $\frac{1}{6} < \frac{2}{9}$.

Write both fractions as equivalent fractions with the same denominator. Use the LCM of 6 and 9 as your denominator.

Mixed numbers and improper fractions

Fractions that are less than a whole unit are called **proper fractions**.

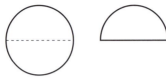

In the diagram there are one and a half circles or three half-circles. One and a half is written as $1\frac{1}{2}$ and is called a **mixed number**.

Three halves is written as $\frac{3}{2}$ and is called an **improper fraction**.

$3 \div 2$ and $\frac{3}{2}$ mean the same thing.

There are $1\frac{1}{2}$ twos in 3 so $\frac{3}{2} = 1\frac{1}{2}$.

> A mixed number contains a whole number and a fraction.

> In an improper fraction the numerator is bigger than the denominator.

Example 3

a Write $\frac{17}{5}$ as a mixed number.

b Write $2\frac{1}{3}$ as an improper fraction.

> $\frac{17}{5}$ and $17 \div 5$ mean the same thing.

a $17 \div 5 = 3$ remainder 2

so $\frac{17}{5} = 3 + \frac{2}{5} = 3\frac{2}{5}$

> To change an improper fraction to a mixed number, divide the numerator by the denominator to give the number of units; the remainder is the number of fractional parts.

b $2\frac{1}{3} = \frac{6+1}{3} = \frac{7}{3}$

> To change a mixed number to an improper fraction, multiply the units by the denominator and add the result to the numerator.

Exam practice 3B

1 Write each of the following improper fractions as a mixed number.

   a $\frac{9}{4}$ **b** $\frac{53}{10}$ **c** $\frac{43}{8}$ **d** $\frac{69}{11}$

2 Write each of these mixed numbers as an improper fraction.

   a $1\frac{1}{4}$ **b** $2\frac{1}{3}$ **c** $3\frac{1}{4}$ **d** $6\frac{3}{4}$

3 Work out each of these divisions. Give your answer as a mixed number.

   a $33 \div 8$ **b** $27 \div 6$ **c** $42 \div 10$ **d** $17 \div 9$

4 Express $\frac{5}{7}$ and $\frac{2}{3}$ as equivalent fractions with the same denominator.
   Which is the larger: $\frac{5}{7}$ or $\frac{2}{3}$?

5 **a** Which is the larger: $\frac{2}{9}$ of a sum of money or $\frac{1}{7}$ of it?

   b Which is the smaller: $\frac{2}{7}$ of a box of sweets or $\frac{3}{8}$ of it?

   c Which is the larger: $\frac{4}{5}$ of a loaf of bread or $\frac{6}{7}$ of it?

> Choose the LCM of 9 and 7 as your denominator.

6 a Write the fractions $\frac{1}{4}$ and $\frac{2}{7}$ in order of size, smallest first.

   b Write the fractions $\frac{2}{3}$, $\frac{5}{6}$ and $\frac{3}{5}$ in order of size, smallest first

   c Write the fractions $\frac{2}{5}$, $\frac{1}{8}$, $\frac{19}{20}$ and $\frac{7}{10}$ in order of size, smallest first.

7 Write the fractions $\frac{1}{3}$, $\frac{5}{6}$, $\frac{1}{2}$ and $\frac{7}{12}$ in order of size, largest first.

8 Using the figures 1, 2, 3, 4 and 5 make as many fractions as you can with a single digit on the top and a different single digit on the bottom that are

   a less than $\frac{1}{2}$ b exactly $\frac{1}{2}$ c between $\frac{1}{2}$ and 1.

3.3 Expressing one quantity as a fraction of another

To find one quantity as a fraction of another,
- write both quantities in the same units
- put the first quantity over the second quantity
- simplify the fraction.

You cannot find 2 hours as a fraction of £10 because they are not the same kind of quantity so cannot be given in the same units.

Example 4

Find 15 minutes as a fraction of $1\frac{1}{2}$ hours.

$1\frac{1}{2}$ hours = 90 minutes

so 15 minutes is $\frac{15}{90}$ of $1\frac{1}{2}$ hours.

$\frac{15}{90} = \frac{1}{6}$, so 15 minutes is $\frac{1}{6}$ of $1\frac{1}{2}$ hours.

$\div 15$

Exam practice 3C

Give all answers as fractions in their simplest form.

1 Len took 4 chocolates from a box of 24. What fraction was this?

2 Sally was driven 180 miles. She slept for 108 miles. What fraction of the journey was she asleep?

3 4500 of the 12 000 people who attended a concert were under 15. What fraction was this?

4 a Find 36 cm as a fraction of 144 cm.
   b Find 65 cm as a fraction of 3 metres.
   c Find 24p as a fraction of £5.

5   Each week, Jon saved £1.50 of his £4 pocket money.
    What fraction of his pocket money did Jon save?

6   What fraction of one hour is
    a   1 minute   b   10 minutes   c   45 minutes   d   36 minutes?

7   Fred's journey to school costs 55p on one bus and 35p on
    another bus.
    a   Find the total cost of his journey.
    b   What fraction of the total cost is the fare on the second bus?

8   Andrew has a 25 hectare field. He plants 15 hectares with wheat.
    What fraction of the field does he plant with wheat?

9   Simon gets £4.80 a week pocket money. He spends £2.70.
    What fraction of his pocket money is left?

10 When she went on holiday, Carol's luggage weighed 18 kg.
    When she got home her luggage weighed 15 kg.
    What was the weight of her luggage on return as a fraction of
    the weight of her luggage when she went away?

11 This pumpkin weighed 6 kg before it was carved.
    It now weighs 2 kg.
    What fraction of its weight was cut away?

12 In a quiz Pat scored 20 out of 80 on Section A and 54 out of 60
    on Section B.
    What fraction of the total score did Pat get?

3.4 Addition and subtraction

Fractions with the same denominator can be added or subtracted by
adding or subtracting their numerators.

Fractions with different denominators must be written as equivalent
fractions with the same denominator before they can be added or
subtracted.

Example 5

Find $\frac{3}{4} - \frac{2}{3}$.

$$\frac{3}{4} - \frac{2}{3} = \frac{9}{12} - \frac{8}{12}$$
$$= \frac{1}{12}$$

Write both fractions as equivalent fractions
with the same denominator. Choose the
LCM of the two denominators.

You can add and subtract mixed numbers by writing them as
improper fractions.

Example 6

Find **a** $2\frac{1}{2} + 1\frac{3}{5}$ **b** $2\frac{1}{2} - 1\frac{3}{5}$.

a $2\frac{1}{2} + 1\frac{3}{5} = \frac{5}{2} + \frac{8}{5}$

Write each mixed number as an improper fraction.

$= \frac{25}{10} + \frac{16}{10}$

Write as equivalent fractions with denominator 10.

$= \frac{41}{10}$

Write your answer as a mixed number.

$= 4\frac{1}{10}$

You do not always have to use improper fractions. You can deal with the whole numbers first:

$2\frac{1}{2} + 1\frac{3}{5} = 2 + \frac{1}{2} + 1 + \frac{3}{5} = 3 + \frac{1}{2} + \frac{3}{5} = 3 + \frac{5}{10} + \frac{6}{10} = 3\frac{11}{10} = 3 + 1\frac{1}{10} = 4\frac{1}{10}$

b $2\frac{1}{2} - 1\frac{3}{5} = \frac{5}{2} - \frac{8}{5}$

Alternatively

$2\frac{1}{2} - 1\frac{3}{5} = 1 + \frac{1}{2} - \frac{3}{5} = 1 + \frac{5}{10} - \frac{6}{10} = 1 - \frac{1}{10} = \frac{10}{10} - \frac{1}{10} = \frac{9}{10}$

$= \frac{25}{10} - \frac{16}{10}$

$= \frac{9}{10}$

Exam practice 3D

1 Find each of these as a fraction in its lowest terms:
   a $\frac{2}{5} + \frac{1}{4}$ b $\frac{1}{4} + \frac{7}{10}$ c $\frac{7}{10} - \frac{1}{2}$
   d $\frac{2}{3} - \frac{1}{2}$ e $\frac{1}{3} + \frac{1}{5}$ f $\frac{5}{6} - \frac{2}{3}$

2 Find each of these as a fraction in its lowest terms:
   a $\frac{3}{5} + \frac{2}{25} - \frac{3}{20}$ b $\frac{1}{3} - \frac{5}{18} + \frac{4}{9}$ c $2\frac{1}{4} + \frac{4}{5}$

3 Find each of these as a fraction in its lowest terms:
   a $3\frac{1}{4} + 1\frac{1}{5}$ b $2\frac{1}{2} + 1\frac{3}{4}$ c $1\frac{3}{5} - \frac{1}{2}$
   d $3\frac{1}{3} - 1\frac{1}{2}$ e $2\frac{1}{4} - 1\frac{2}{3}$ f $1\frac{1}{3} - \frac{3}{4}$

4 Find each of these as a fraction in its lowest terms:
   a $\frac{4}{5} - \frac{7}{10} + \frac{1}{2}$ b $4\frac{1}{5} - 5\frac{1}{2} + 1\frac{3}{10}$ c $6\frac{1}{3} - 1\frac{2}{5} + 1\frac{8}{15}$

5 The sum of two fractions is $\frac{13}{18}$. One of the fractions is $\frac{1}{12}$.
   What is the other?

6 Stan has a $5\frac{1}{4}$ metre length of cloth.
   Dilly buys $2\frac{3}{4}$ metres of it.
   How much does Stan have left.

7 Tim has two lengths of skirting board.
   One is $3\frac{1}{4}$ metres long and the other is $4\frac{7}{8}$ metres.
   He needs $7\frac{5}{8}$ metres.
   How much will he have over?

8 The ceiling of a room is $8\frac{1}{2}$ feet high.
   A picture, which is $2\frac{1}{4}$ feet high, hangs on a wall.
   The bottom of the picture is $4\frac{5}{8}$ feet from the floor.
   Work out the distance from the top of the picture to the ceiling.

Mini coursework task

You cannot use improper fractions in this activity.

Look at the digits 2, 3, 4, 5, 6 and 7.

a   Use two of these digits to make a fraction that is
  i   as large as possible   ii   as small as possible.
b   Use two of the digits on the top and two on the bottom to make a fraction that is
  i   as large as possible   ii   as small as possible.
c   Use two pairs of these digits to make two equivalent fractions.
d   Make two fractions with a difference that is
  i   as large as possible   ii   as small as possible.

> You can use the digits to make fractions such as $\frac{2}{3}$ or $\frac{6}{7}$.

> No digit can be used more than once in the same fraction, so $\frac{23}{37}$ is not allowed because 3 is used twice.

> Each digit can be used only once. The numerator and denominator must have the same number of digits.

3.5 Fractions of a quantity

To find a fraction of a quantity, you divide by the denominator, then multiply the answer by the numerator.

Example 7

Find $\frac{2}{3}$ of the number of tiles on this floor.

There are 12 tiles.

$\frac{1}{3}$ of 12 = 12 ÷ 3 = 4

so $\frac{2}{3}$ of 12 = 4 × 2 = 8.

> A third means one of 3 equal sized parts, so divide these twelve tiles into 3 equal parts. You want two of these parts so multiply by 2.

Example 8

Find $\frac{5}{8}$ of £48.

$\frac{1}{8}$ of £48 = £48 ÷ 8 = £6

so $\frac{5}{8}$ of £48 = 5 × £6 = £30.

> First find $\frac{1}{8}$, then multiply your answer by 5.

Exam practice 3E

1 Find: a $\frac{3}{9}$ of 99 miles   b $\frac{7}{16}$ of 48 litres
           c $\frac{4}{9}$ of 63 kilometres   d $\frac{5}{6}$ of 1 day
           e $\frac{3}{5}$ of 235p   f $\frac{4}{7}$ of 294 cm
           g $\frac{4}{5}$ of 1 year of 365 days   h $\frac{7}{12}$ of 1 hour.

> Use 1 day = 24 hours and
> 1 hour = 60 minutes.

2 Find:
   a $\frac{2}{7}$ of a week   b $\frac{1}{4}$ of £24   c $\frac{1}{3}$ of 1 hour
   d $\frac{2}{3}$ of a minute   e $\frac{1}{5}$ of £5   f $\frac{3}{4}$ of 36 cm
   g $\frac{1}{9}$ of 27 cm   h $\frac{5}{8}$ of 36 ft   i $\frac{3}{7}$ of £49
   j $\frac{3}{5}$ of 1 year   k $\frac{2}{5}$ of £85   l $\frac{7}{8}$ of £96.

> Convert to smaller units if you need to. Remember to give units in your answer.

3   In a school election Peter got $\frac{5}{12}$ of the votes and Sue got $\frac{2}{5}$.
    60 people were entitled to vote.
    a   How many people voted for **i** Peter **ii** Sue?
    b   How many people did not vote for Peter or Sue?

4   Sally has a 60 metre ball of string.
    She used $\frac{3}{5}$ of it on Monday and $\frac{1}{4}$ of it on Tuesday.
    a   What length of string did she use **i** on Monday **ii** on Tuesday?
    b   What length remained?

5   Sam pays £560 for 150 DVDs.
    He sells $\frac{2}{5}$ of them for £8 each.
    He sells the rest of the DVDs for £4 each.
    a   Work out how much he gets from selling the DVDs.
    b   How much profit did he make?
    c   Express this profit as a fraction of what he originally paid for
        the DVDs.

6   Claire took part in a 12 kilometre cross country race.
    She ran $\frac{1}{4}$ of the way.
    a   How far did she still have to go?
    She walked for $\frac{2}{3}$ of the remaining distance before she stopped
    for a rest.
    s   How far did she walk before she rested?
    c   How far did she still have to go?

7   Robin is an old lady. She lived one-sixth of her life as a girl and
    one-fifteenth as a youth. She was married for half her life and
    has been a widow for twenty-four years.
    How old is Robin now?

8   Donna, Julian and Maria need £5360 to open a hairdressing salon.
    Donna contributes $\frac{7}{20}$, Julian $\frac{3}{10}$ and Maria the remainder.
    How much does each person contribute?

9   There were two candidates in a local election.
    $\frac{4}{7}$ of the electorate voted for Brown and $\frac{2}{7}$ voted for Charles.
    Brown's majority was 686.
    a   How many voted for Charles?
    b   How many voted for Brown?
    c   How many could have voted?

10 In Year 11 three-quarters of the boys play soccer and two-fifths
    play rugby.
    One-fifth play both games.
    Four boys play neither game.
    How many boys are there in Year 11?

11 There are 28 students in a class.
    Of these $\frac{3}{4}$ take geography, $\frac{1}{2}$ take history and 8 take both
    subjects.
    How many students take neither subject?

3.6 Multiplying fractions

To multiply fractions, multiply the numerators together and multiply the denominators together.

You can multiply mixed numbers by writing them as improper fractions.

Example 9

Find **a** $2\frac{1}{2} \times \frac{3}{4}$ **b** $1\frac{1}{2} \times 2\frac{2}{3}$ **c** $\frac{3}{7} \times \frac{5}{6} \times \frac{14}{15}$.

a $2\frac{1}{2} \times \frac{3}{4} = \frac{5}{2} \times \frac{3}{4} = \frac{5 \times 3}{2 \times 4} = \frac{15}{8} = 1\frac{7}{8}$

b $1\frac{1}{2} \times 2\frac{2}{3} = \frac{3}{2} \times \frac{8}{3} = \frac{\cancel{3} \times \cancel{8}^{4}}{\cancel{2} \times \cancel{3}} = \frac{4}{1} = 4$

> You can cancel common factors before you multiply the numerators and denominators.

c $\frac{\cancel{3}^{1}}{7} \times \frac{\cancel{5}^{1}}{\cancel{6}^{2}} \times \frac{\cancel{14}^{2}}{\cancel{15}^{3}} = \frac{1 \times 1 \times \cancel{2}}{1 \times \cancel{2} \times 3} = \frac{1}{3}$

Reciprocals

If the **product** of two numbers is 1 then each number is called the **reciprocal** of the other.

The reciprocal of a fraction is found by turning the fraction upside down.
To find the reciprocal of a mixed number write it as an improper fraction, then turn the fraction upside down.

The reciprocal of a number is 1 divided by that number.
0 does not have a reciprocal because you cannot divide by 0.

> $\frac{1}{4}$ is the reciprocal of 4 and 4 is the reciprocal of $\frac{1}{4}$ because $\frac{1}{4} \times 4 = \frac{1}{4} \times \frac{4}{1} = 1$.

> $1\frac{1}{3} = \frac{4}{3}$
> So the reciprocal of $1\frac{1}{3}$ is $\frac{3}{4}$.

Dividing by a fraction

To divide by a fraction, multiply by its reciprocal.

> The diagram shows that there are two $\frac{1}{4}$s in $\frac{1}{2}$ so $\frac{1}{2} \div \frac{1}{4} = 2$.
> The reciprocal of $\frac{1}{4}$ is 4.
> $\frac{1}{2} \div \frac{1}{4} = \frac{1}{2} \times 4 = \frac{1}{2} \times \frac{4}{1} = 2$.

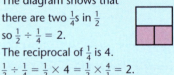

Example 10

Find **a** $2\frac{2}{3} \div \frac{4}{5}$ **b** $2\frac{1}{2} \div 5$.

a $2\frac{2}{3} \div \frac{4}{5} = \frac{8}{3} \times \frac{5}{4}$

> Write mixed numbers as improper fractions.

$= \frac{\cancel{8}^{2} \times 5}{3 \times \cancel{4}_{1}} = \frac{10}{3} = 3\frac{1}{3}$

b $2\frac{1}{2} \div 5 = \frac{5}{2} \div \frac{5}{1}$

> Dividing by 5 is the same as dividing by $\frac{5}{1}$.

$= \frac{5}{2} \times \frac{1}{5} = \frac{\cancel{5}^{1} \times 1}{2 \times \cancel{5}_{1}} = \frac{1}{2}$

Exam practice 3F

1 Find:

  a $\frac{2}{5} \times \frac{1}{3}$ b $\frac{2}{7} \times \frac{3}{7}$ c $\frac{5}{6} \times \frac{1}{4}$ d $\frac{7}{9} \times \frac{2}{9}$

  e $\frac{7}{8} \times \frac{4}{21}$ f $\frac{3}{4} \times \frac{16}{21}$ g $\frac{3}{10} \times \frac{5}{9}$ h $\frac{4}{5} \times \frac{15}{16}$

  i $\frac{7}{8} \times \frac{16}{35}$ j $\frac{4}{15} \times \frac{25}{64}$ k $\frac{21}{22} \times \frac{11}{27}$ l $\frac{10}{11} \times \frac{33}{35}$

2 Work out: a $\frac{3}{4} \times \frac{5}{9} \times \frac{8}{15}$ b $\frac{2}{10} \times \frac{5}{6} \times \frac{6}{7}$

3 Work out:

  a $2\frac{1}{2} \times \frac{2}{5}$ b $3\frac{3}{4} \times \frac{3}{10}$ c $5\frac{2}{3} \times \frac{30}{34}$ d $2\frac{1}{5} \times \frac{5}{22}$

  e $\frac{7}{12} \times 2\frac{2}{5}$ f $8\frac{1}{3} \times 3\frac{3}{5}$ g $5\frac{1}{2} \times \frac{9}{11}$ h $2\frac{2}{7} \times 8\frac{3}{4}$

  i $4 \times 3\frac{3}{8}$ j $3\frac{1}{8} \times 16$ k $2\frac{2}{7} \times 14$ l $3\frac{3}{5} \times 10$

> Write each mixed number as an improper fraction first.

4 Find: a $\frac{3}{4} \times \frac{6}{7}$ b $2\frac{1}{2} \times \frac{7}{10}$ c $5\frac{1}{3} \times \frac{5}{8}$

5 Write down the reciprocal of:

  a $\frac{3}{5}$ b $\frac{7}{9}$ c 4 d 6

  e $2\frac{1}{2}$ f $3\frac{1}{4}$ g $2\frac{3}{4}$

6 Work out:

  a $\frac{21}{32} \div \frac{7}{8}$ b $\frac{8}{21} \div \frac{4}{7}$ c $4 \div \frac{2}{3}$ d $2 \div \frac{2}{5}$

  e $5 \div \frac{3}{4}$ f $3\frac{1}{8} \div 3\frac{3}{4}$ g $6\frac{4}{9} \div 1\frac{1}{3}$ h $9 \div \frac{3}{13}$

  i $\frac{3}{4} \div 30$ j $\frac{35}{42} \div \frac{5}{6}$ k $\frac{3}{28} \div \frac{9}{14}$ l $8 \div 1\frac{1}{3}$

7 Calculate:

  a $8\frac{3}{4} \div 12\frac{1}{2}$ b $9\frac{3}{4} \div 1\frac{5}{8}$ c $3\frac{3}{10} \div 8\frac{4}{5}$ d $6\frac{3}{4} \div 7$

8 Divide: a $1\frac{11}{21}$ by $9\frac{1}{7}$ b $10\frac{5}{6}$ by $6\frac{1}{2}$.

9 How many $2\frac{1}{4}$s are there in $13\frac{1}{2}$?

10 Les has $3\frac{3}{4}$ metres of cloth. He cut off $\frac{2}{3}$ of it.
   How much is this?

11 The length of a piece of string is $2\frac{1}{2}$ metres.
   Evan cut off $\frac{3}{5}$ of it.
   a What length does Evan cut off?
   b What length remains?

12 A rectangular sheet of metal measures $1\frac{1}{4}$ metres by $\frac{3}{4}$ metres.
   Jon cuts $\frac{1}{2}$ off the length and $\frac{1}{3}$ off the width.
   What are the measurements of the sheet that remains?

13 How many pieces of tape, each $3\frac{3}{4}$ cm long, can be cut from a roll
   60 cm long?

14 An empty jar holds $\frac{3}{8}$ litre.
   How many similar jars can be filled from a barrel holding
   21 litres?

15 The area of a rectangular blackboard is $8\frac{3}{4}$ square metres.
It is $1\frac{2}{3}$ metres wide. How long is it?

> The area of a rectangle is the length × the width.

16 It takes $3\frac{1}{3}$ minutes to fill $\frac{3}{8}$ of a water storage tank.
How long will it take to fill the whole tank?

17 When the larger of two fractions is divided by the smaller, the result is $1\frac{7}{18}$.
The smaller fraction is $2\frac{2}{5}$.
Work out the larger fraction.

18 A cylindrical rod is $5\frac{1}{2}$ m long.
Cylinders, each $\frac{3}{16}$ m high, are cut off.
a Work out the largest number of complete cylinders that can be cut off.
b What is the length of the piece that is wasted?

Mini coursework task

The fraction $\frac{6729}{13\,458}$ simplifies to $\frac{1}{2}$.

Using the digits 1, 2, 3, 4, 5, 6, 7, 8, 9 once each find a fraction which is equivalent to $\frac{1}{3}$.

Summary of key points

- You can find equivalent fractions by multiplying the numerator and denominator by the same number.
- You can simplify fractions by dividing the numerator and denominator by a common factor.
- You can add and subtract fractions by changing them to equivalent fractions with the same denominator.
- You can find one quantity as a fraction of another by making sure that they are in the same units, then writing the first quantity over the second.
- $15 \div 4$ and $\frac{15}{14}$ mean the same thing.
- You can compare the size of fractions by writing them as equivalent fractions with the same denominator and comparing their numerators.
- To find a fraction of a quantity divide by the denominator and multiply by the numerator.
- You multiply and divide with whole numbers by writing them as fractions with denominator 1.
- To multiply a fraction by a fraction you multiply the numerators together and multiply the denominators together.
- To divide by a fraction you multiply by its reciprocal.
- Convert mixed numbers into improper fractions before carrying out calculations.

Most candidates who get GRADE C or above can:
- solve problems using mixed numbers.

Glossary

Cancel	find a simpler equivalent fraction by dividing the numerator and denominator by the same number
Denominator	the bottom number in a fraction
Equivalent fraction	an equal sized fraction with a different denominator and numerator
Fraction	part of a quantity
Improper fraction	a fraction whose numerator is larger than its denominator
Lowest possible terms	when a fraction has been simplified as far as possible
Mixed number	a number that contains a whole number and a fraction, e.g. $3\frac{1}{3}$
Numerator	the top number in a fraction
Product	the result of multiplying two numbers together
Proper fraction	a fraction that is less than 1 whole unit, e.g. $\frac{4}{5}$
Reciprocal	the number given when 1 is divided by that number
Simplifying a fraction	dividing the numerator and denominator by the same number to get an equivalent fraction with a smaller numerator and denominator

4 Decimals

This chapter will show you:
- ✓ the meaning of decimal places
- ✓ how to write a decimal as a fraction
- ✓ how to add or subtract decimal numbers
- ✓ how to multiply or divide a decimal number by a whole number or another decimal number
- ✓ how to write a number correct to a given number of decimal places
- ✓ how to write a fraction as a decimal
- ✓ that some fractions give recurring decimals
- ✓ how to convert a recurring decimal to a fraction

Before you start you need to know:
- ✓ how to add and subtract whole numbers
- ✓ how to do short and long division
- ✓ how to multiply fractions together
- ✓ how to multiply by whole numbers

4.1 Place value

The position of a digit in a number is called its **place value**. It tells you the value of that digit.

Mixed numbers can be written as decimal numbers. They are written with a decimal point after the units.

This column represents hundredths. It is called the second **decimal place**.

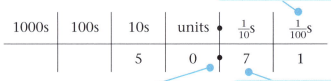

1000s	100s	10s	units	$\frac{1}{10}$s	$\frac{1}{100}$s
		5	0	7	1

This is the decimal point.

This column represents tenths. It is called the first decimal place.

Did you know

that the word decimal comes from the latin word *decimus* meaning 'tenth'?

The number is 50.71
In words you write fifty point seven one.

You can compare the size of two or more decimals by looking at the digits in each place value.

Example 1

Which is the larger, 4.67 or 4.632?

4.67 is larger than 4.632.

Do not assume that the number with the most digits is the larger number.
Look first at the number of units – they are the same.
Next look at the number of tenths – they are also the same.
Finally look at the number of hundredths – 7 is larger than 3, so 4.67 is larger than 4.632. (You can think of this as 670 > 632.)

Converting decimals to fractions

The positions of the figures after the decimal point tell you their value. You can use this to write decimal numbers as **fractions**.

Example 2

a Write 0.15 as a fraction.   **b** Write 1.025 as a fraction.

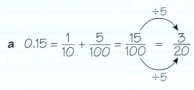

a $0.15 = \dfrac{1}{10} + \dfrac{5}{100} = \dfrac{15}{100} = \dfrac{3}{20}$

Check: $\dfrac{3}{20} = 3 \div 20 = 0.15$

b $1.025 = 1 + \dfrac{2}{100} + \dfrac{5}{1000}$

$= 1 + \dfrac{20}{1000} + \dfrac{5}{1000} = 1\dfrac{25}{1000}$

$= 1\dfrac{1}{40}$

> 0.15 means
> $\dfrac{1}{10} + \dfrac{5}{100} = \dfrac{10 + 5}{100}$.

Adding and subtracting decimals

Decimals can be added or subtracted in the same way as whole numbers. You add hundredths to hundredths, tenths to tenths, and so on.

Example 3

Work out $1.6 + 3 + 0.05$.

```
   1.60
   3.00
+  0.05
-------
   4.65
```

> Write the numbers in a column with the decimal points under one another. Add 0s so that each number has the same number of decimal places.

Example 4

Calculate $3.5 - 1.06$.

```
   3.50
-  1.06
-------
   2.44
```

> Write the numbers in a column and write 3.5 as 3.50 to give 2 decimal places.

Exam practice 4A

1 Express as a decimal   a $\frac{4}{10}$ b $\frac{15}{100}$ c $\frac{63}{100}$ d $\frac{3}{10}$.

2 Write down the value of the figure 7 in each of the following numbers.
   a 3.07   b 73   c 30.07
   d 2.74   e 57.5   f 0.007

> The first place to the right of the decimal point gives tenths, the second place hundredths, and so on.

3 Which is the larger of the two numbers?
   a 3.57 or 3.59   b 25.64 or 25.46   c 4.88 or 5

4 Which is the smaller of the two numbers?
   a 6.74 or 6.71   b 85.37 or 85.73   c 6.33 or 6

5 Write each set of numbers in order of size, largest first.
   a 12.6, 14.09, 12.55, 13.75   b 7.555, 7.5, 7.05, 7.55

6 Write each decimal as a fraction in its simplest form.
   a 0.2   b 0.5   c 0.06
   d 0.7   e 0.8   f 0.025

> Remember that 0.4 is $\frac{4}{10}$, 0.04 is $\frac{4}{100}$, 0.44 is $\frac{44}{100}$ and so on.
> Remember also that to give a fraction in its simplest form means you have to cancel it as much as possible.

7 Work out:
   a 1.6 + 0.3   b 2.3 + 0.05   c 2.8 − 1
   d 1.6 − 0.22   e 0.24 + 1.7   f 1.77 + 3.9
   g 0.5 − 0.04   h 2.44 − 1.74

8 Find the value of:
   a 3 − 1.7   b 0.7 − 0.38
   c 1.2 − 0.07   d 8.04 − 3.27
   e 2.3 + 0.4 + 7.8   f 7.5 + 1.44 + 3.06
   g 6 − 3.8 + 1.5   h 7.2 + 2.7 − 5.6

9 What is the perimeter of this rectangle?

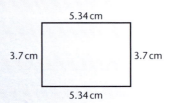

> **Perimeter** means the total length of the edges.

10 The perimeter of a quadrilateral is 15.34 cm.
    The lengths of three of the sides are 3.6 cm, 4.88 cm and 4.52 cm.
    Work out the length of the fourth side.

> A **quadrilateral** is a shape bounded by four straight lines.

11 The bill for three meals was £58.
    One meal cost £14.42 and the another meal cost £15.78.
    What was the cost of the third meal?

12 A stick of wood is 28.3 centimetres long.
    Three pieces are cut off this stick.
    Their lengths are 8.3 cm, 2.8 cm and 7.7 cm.
    What length is left?

13 The distances a lorry travelled between deliveries were 31.2 km,
    27.5 km, 9.9 km and 16.3 km.
    This is the display at the last
    delivery point.

Read the question
carefully. Make sure
you understand what
you are being asked
to find.

    What did it show at the first delivery
    point?

14 A piece of wood is 20.2 mm thick.
    It is planed to make it smooth.
    The first planing takes 1.08 mm off the thickness.
    The second planing takes another 0.34 mm off it.
    Work out the new thickness.

15 A length of metal passes through a set of rollers.
    The first pass reduces its thickness by 0.44 mm.
    The second pass reduces its thickness by 0.33 mm and the third
    pass by 0.25 mm. The metal is now 8.2 mm thick.
    How thick was it to start with?

16 Misha bought four magazines and a newspaper.
    Two of the magazines cost £2.75 each and the other two
    magazines cost £3.15 each.
    Misha paid with a £20 note and got £7.60 change.
    How much did the newspaper cost?

17 The perimeter of this quadrilateral is 37 cm.
    The shortest side is 7.2 cm long and the next shortest side is
    2.36 cm longer than this.
    The length of the longest side is one-and-a-half times the length
    of the shortest side.
    How long is the fourth side?

4.2 Multiplying and dividing decimals

When a number is multiplied by 10, 100, 1000,... the digits move
1, 2, 3,... places to the left.

Example 5

Find: **a** 0.45×100 **b** 0.45×1000

    a $0.45 \times 100 = 45$

    b $0.45 \times 1000 = 450$

When a number is
multiplied by 10,
the tens become
hundreds, units
become tens, tenths
become units, and so
on. The digits move
up one place value.

When a number is divided by 10, 100, 1000,...the figures move 1, 2, 3,... places to the right.

> When a number is divided by 10, the tens become units, units become tenths and so on. So the digits move down one place value.

Example 6

Find: **a** $45 \div 10$ **b** $45 \div 1000$

a $45 \div 10 = 4.5$

b $45 \div 1000 = 0.045$

You can multiply and divide a decimal by a whole number in the same way that you multiply and divide a whole number.

Example 7

Find: **a** 1.3×2 **b** 1.3×200 **c** $2.7 \div 2$ **d** $2.7 \div 200$

a $1.3 \times 2 = 2.6$

b $1.3 \times 200 = 1.3 \times 2 \times 100 = 2.6 \times 100 = 260$

> To multiply by 200, first multiply by 2, then by 100.

c $2.7 \div 2 = 1.35$ $\dfrac{1.35}{2\overline{)2.70}}$

> Add 0s to continue the division.

d $2.7 \div 200 = 2.7 \div 2 \div 100 = 1.35 \div 100 = 0.0135$

> Divide by 2 then by 100.

When you divide a whole number by another whole number, you can use decimals to continue the division.

Example 8

Find $135 \div 8$.

$135 \div 8 = 16.875$ $\dfrac{16.875}{8\overline{)135.000}}$

> Put in a decimal point and add zeros to continue the division.

You can also divide any number by a decimal. Write the calculation as a fraction and find an equivalent fraction with a whole number **denominator**.

Example 9

Find: **a** $2.8 \div 0.2$ **b** $44.8 \div 0.08$

a $2.8 \div 0.2 = \dfrac{2.8}{0.2} = \dfrac{2.8 \times 10}{0.2 \times 10} = \dfrac{28}{2} = 14$

b $44.8 \div 0.08 = \dfrac{44.8}{0.08} = \dfrac{44.8 \times 100}{0.08 \times 100} = \dfrac{4480}{8} = 560$

You can use this rule to multiply decimals:

| Ignore the decimal points and just multiply the numbers. | → | Count the decimal places in the calculation. | → | Put this number of decimal places in the answer. |

The sum of the numbers of decimal places in the calculation is equal to the number of decimal places in the result.

The rule for multiplying decimals comes from fractions:

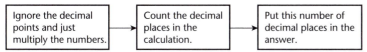

$$1.6 \times 0.02 = \tfrac{16}{10} \times \tfrac{2}{100} = \tfrac{32}{1000} = 0.032$$

One place after the decimal point.   Two places after the decimal point.   Three places after the decimal point.

Exam practice 4B

1 Work in your head and write down the value of
   a 2.5×100 **b** 0.066×10 **c** 24.4×1000 **d** 0.1×100
   e 0.3×300 **f** 1.6×20 **g** 1.2×30 **h** 0.7×200.

2 Work in your head and write down the value of
   a $4.6 \div 10$ **b** $0.85 \div 1000$ **c** $12 \div 10$
   d $9.6 \div 100$ **e** $1.5 \div 50$ **f** $14.4 \div 120$
   g $25 \div 5000$ **h** $0.84 \div 40$.

3 Work in your head and write down the value of
   a 1.6×0.3 **b** 0.12×0.2 **c** 0.22×0.04 **d** 1.05×0.002
   e 1.2×0.1 **f** $(0.1)^2$ **g** 45×0.1 **h** $(0.01)^2$.

4 Work in your head and write down the value of
   a $0.3 \div 0.1$ **b** $2 \div 0.2$ **c** $1.4 \div 0.07$ **d** $0.36 \div 1.2$
   e $9.9 \div 0.01$ **f** $26.7 \div 0.08$ **g** $10.5 \div 1.5$ **h** $1.08 \div 1.2$.

> Never try to divide by the decimal before changing it to a whole number.

5 Work out:
   a 2.56×1.2 **b** $3.6 \div 0.12$ **c** 4.5×0.03
   d $0.056 \div 0.8$ **e** $8.4 \div 21$ **f** 1.33×0.2
   g $4.5 \div 1.5$ **h** 0.7×6.3 **i** 400×0.6
   j $500 \div 0.04$ **k** 1200×0.001 **l** $14.7 \div 0.2$

6 Find: **a** $(0.2)^3$ **b** $\dfrac{0.4}{(0.2)^3}$ **c** $2.25 - (1.2)^2$

7   **a**   Find the cost of 26 books at £6.55 each.
     b   Find the cost of 5.4 m of wood at 35p per metre.

8   A company employs 8 people.
   Each person is paid £372.55 a week.
   Work out the weekly wage bill for the 8 employees.

9   Wood costs 2.5p per cubic centimetre.
   Find the cost of 85.4 cubic centimetres of wood.

10   16 coins are placed in a pile.
    Each coin is 1.23 millimetres thick.
    Work out the height of the pile.

11   A piece of wire, 12.55 metres long, is cut into 50 pieces of equal
    length. How long is each piece?

12   Given that $8288 \div 37 = 224$, find the exact value of

    a $82.88 \div 3.7$ **b** $\dfrac{8.288}{0.224}$

13   Given that $1.5^2 \times 0.3^2 = 0.2025$, find the exact value of
    $20.25 \div 15^2$.

4.3 Rounding to a given number of decimal places

You can round a number to a given number of decimal places.

**To give a number correct to a number of decimal places,
draw a line after that decimal place and look at the digit
after the line.**

If it is less than 5, round down.

If it is 5 or more, round up.

> Giving a number to the nearest tenth is called **rounding** to one decimal place. Giving a number to the nearest hundredth is called rounding to two decimal places.

Example 10

Give 1.3847 correct to

a the nearest tenth   **b** two decimal places.

    a   1.3|847 = 1.4 correct to 1 d.p.

    b   1.38|47 = 1.38 correct to 2 d.p.

> To the nearest tenth means to one decimal place. d.p. is short for decimal place.

Converting fractions to decimals

To write a fraction as a decimal, divide the **numerator** by the denominator.

Example 11

Write $\frac{3}{8}$ as a decimal.

$\frac{3}{8}$ means $3 \div 8$.

$$\frac{3}{8} = 0.375$$

$$\begin{array}{r} 0.375 \\ 8\overline{)3.000} \end{array}$$

Exam practice 4C

1 Write:

   a 298.2 to the nearest ten   b 39.78 to the nearest unit

   c 139.78 to the nearest unit   d 0.479 to the nearest unit

   e 375 to the nearest hundred   f 0.6942 correct to 2 d.p.

   g 40.378 correct to 2 d.p.   h 28.75 correct to 1 d.p.

2 Write:

   a 13.479 correct to 1 d.p.   b 0.9999 correct to 2 d.p.

   c 77.99841 correct to 3 d.p.   d 2.2525 correct to 3 d.p.

   e 1.002793 correct to 4 d.p.   f 0.0507702 correct to 5 d.p.

3 Express each fraction as a decimal.

   a $\frac{1}{5}$ b $\frac{1}{8}$ c $\frac{3}{4}$ d $\frac{3}{5}$

   e $\frac{3}{20}$ f $\frac{1}{4}$ g $\frac{7}{8}$ h $\frac{6}{25}$

   > Divide the top by the bottom and continue the division until it stops.

4 Which is the bigger number?

   a $\frac{2}{5}$ or 0.3   b $\frac{4}{5}$ or 0.78   c $\frac{7}{8}$ or 0.79

   > Convert the fraction to a decimal.

5 Which is the smaller number?

   a $\frac{5}{8}$ or 0.6   b 0.66 or $\frac{2}{3}$ c 1.8 or $\frac{11}{6}$

   > Write the fractions as decimals. You will need to work to 3 decimal places.

6 a Write each fraction as a decimal correct to 3 decimal places.

      $1.57, \frac{5}{3}, 1.49, 1\frac{2}{7}, \frac{15}{11}$

   b Now arrange these numbers in order with the smallest first.

   > Work to 4 decimal places to give your answer correct to 3 decimal places.

7 Arrange these numbers in order of size, the largest first.

      $0.05, \frac{3}{16}, 0.105, \frac{2}{13}, \frac{6}{25}$

A01   8 Doug wrote $\frac{1}{3} = 0.3$.

   Explain why Doug is wrong.

4.4 Recurring decimals

If you try to write $\frac{1}{3}$ as a decimal, you get 0.33333… and so on for ever.

> The digit 3 recurs.

0.33333… is called a **recurring decimal**.
It is written $0.\dot{3}$.

> A dot over a digit means that it recurs.
> So $0.\dot{5}$ means 0.5555555…

Any decimal with a recurring digit or pattern of digits is called a recurring decimal.

When you convert a fraction to a decimal, you will either get an exact decimal, or a recurring decimal.

> $\frac{1}{13}$ = 0.076923076923076… where 076923 recurs.
> You write this as $0.\dot{0}7692\dot{3}$.
> The dots show the pattern of digits that repeat.

You can tell whether a fraction will convert to an exact decimal by looking at the prime factors in its denominator.
Write the fraction in its simplest form, then look at the factors of the denominator. Any combination of 2s and/or 5s gives an exact decimal.

Example 12

Which of the following fractions give an exact decimal?

a $\frac{7}{20}$ **b** $\frac{5}{13}$ **c** $\frac{6}{35}$ **d** $\frac{5}{8}$

> **a** $\frac{7}{20} = \frac{7}{2 \times 2 \times 5}$ so $\frac{7}{20}$ gives an exact decimal.
>
> **b** $\frac{5}{13}$ gives a recurring decimal.
>
> **c** $\frac{6}{35} = \frac{6}{5 \times 7}$ so $\frac{6}{35}$ gives a recurring decimal.
>
> **d** $\frac{5}{8} = \frac{5}{2 \times 2 \times 2}$ so $\frac{5}{8}$ gives an exact decimal.

> Parts **b** and **c** give recurring decimals as the denominators have factors other than 2 and 5.

Converting a recurring decimal to a fraction

You need these facts to convert a recurring decimal to a fraction:

$\frac{1}{9}$ = 0.111 111 111…,

$\frac{1}{99}$ = 0.01 01 01 01…,

$\frac{1}{999}$ = 0.001 001 001…

You need to write the recurring decimal as a **product** of one of these numbers.

> 0.666 666 666… = 6 × 0.111 111 111…
> and 0.0125 125 125… = 125 × 0.0001001001001…
> = 125 × $\frac{1}{10}$ × 0.001001…

Example 13

Convert each recurring decimal to a fraction.
a 0.444 444…   **b** 0.17 17 17 17…
c 0.375 375 375…   **d** $0.0\dot{4}\dot{7}$ **e** $0.1\dot{5}$

a $0.444\,444... = 4 \times 0.1111111... = 4 \times \frac{1}{9} = \frac{4}{9}$

b $0.17\,17\,17\,17... = 17 \times 0.01\,01\,01\,01... = 17 \times \frac{1}{99} = \frac{17}{99}$

c $0.375\,375\,375... = 375 \times 0.001\,001\,001... = 375 \times \frac{1}{999} = \frac{375}{999} = \frac{125}{333}$ Simplify the fraction.

d $0.0\dot{4}\dot{7} = 0.047\,47\,47... = 47 \times 0.001010101...$
$= 47 \times \frac{1}{10} \times 0.01\,01\,01...$ ● —— $0.0010101...$ is $\frac{1}{10}$th of $0.010101...$
$= \frac{47}{10} \times \frac{1}{99} = \frac{47}{990}$

e $0.1\dot{5} = 0.1 + 0.05555...$
$= 0.1 + \frac{1}{10} \times 0.55555...$
$= \frac{1}{10} + \frac{1}{10} \times 5 \times 0.11111...$
$= \frac{1}{10} + \frac{1}{10} \times 5 \times \frac{1}{9} = \frac{1}{10} + \frac{1}{18} = \frac{9+5}{90} = \frac{14}{90} = \frac{7}{45}$

Using algebra

You can convert a recurring decimal to a fraction by multiplying it by a power of 10.
This is an alternative to the numerical method given above.

Powers of 10 are 10, 100, 1000,...

Example 14

Convert each recurring decimal to a fraction.
a $0.444\,444...$ **b** $0.0\dot{4}\dot{7}$
c $0.375\,375\,375...$ **d** $0.1\dot{5}$

a $x = 0.444\,444...$ There is one digit in the recurring pattern so multiply by $10^1 = 10$.
$10x = 4.444\,444...$
$10x - x = 4$ $4.444\,444... - 0.444\,444... = 4$.
$9x = 4$ so $x = \frac{4}{9}$

b $x = 0.047\,47\,47...$ There are two digits in the recurring pattern so multiply by $10^2 = 100$.
$100x = 4.747\,474...$
$100x - x = 4.7$
$99x = 4.7$ so $x = \frac{4.7}{99} = \frac{47}{990}$

c $x = 0.375\,375\,375...$ There are three digits in the recurring pattern so multiply by $10^3 = 1000$.
$1000x = 375.375\,375...$
$1000x - x = 375$
$999x = 375$ so $x = \frac{375}{999} = \frac{125}{333}$ Simplify the fraction.

d $x = 0.155\,555\,555\ldots$ There is one digit in the recurring pattern so multiply by $10^1 = 10$.

$10x = 1.555\,555\,555\ldots$

$10x - x = 1.4$

$9x = 1.4$ so $x = \dfrac{1.4}{9} = \dfrac{14}{90} = \dfrac{7}{45}$

Exam practice 4D

1 Write these recurring decimals using the dot notation:
   a 0.777 777…   **b** 0.033 333…   **c** 0.181 818…
   d 26.353 535…   **e** 0.025 252…   **f** 0.718 718…
   g 6.020 520 520… **h** 1.348 934 89…

2 Find the missing numbers:
   a $0.666\,666\ldots = \square \times 0.111\,111\ldots$
   b $0.191\,919\ldots = \square \times \dfrac{1}{99}$
   c $0.053535\ldots = \square \times \dfrac{1}{10} \times \dfrac{1}{99}$
   d $0.094\,949\ldots = \square \times \dfrac{1}{99}$

The answer to part **d** is a fraction.

3 Write each of the following decimals correct to 6 decimal places.
   a $0.2\dot{6}$ **b** $1.2\dot{5}\dot{7}$ **c** $0.03\dot{1}4\dot{6}$

4 Use dot notation to write each fraction as a decimal.
   a $\dfrac{1}{3}$ **b** $\dfrac{1}{7}$ **c** $\dfrac{1}{13}$ **d** $\dfrac{2}{11}$

Continue the division until you can see the repeating pattern.

5 a Which of these fractions cannot be written as an exact decimal?
         $\dfrac{2}{5}, \dfrac{5}{6}, \dfrac{1}{8}, \dfrac{3}{4}$

   b Write that fraction as a decimal using the dot notation.

6 Express each fraction as a recurring decimal.
   a $\dfrac{2}{3}$ **b** $\dfrac{2}{7}$ **c** $\dfrac{1}{6}$ **d** $\dfrac{4}{15}$ **e** $\dfrac{2}{9}$
   f $\dfrac{1}{12}$ **g** $\dfrac{5}{13}$ **h** $\dfrac{1}{11}$ **i** $\dfrac{3}{11}$ **j** $\dfrac{7}{11}$

You can get the decimals for **i** and **j** from your answer to **h**.

7 A recurring decimal is written $0.\dot{3}1\dot{6}$.
   Write this decimal correct to 9 decimal places.

8 The value of $\dfrac{6}{13}$ as a recurring decimal is $0.\dot{4}6153\dot{8}$.
   Write this decimal correct to 12 decimal places.

9 Use dot notation to write these fractions as decimals.
   a $\dfrac{4}{30}$ **b** $\dfrac{4}{300}$ **c** $\dfrac{4}{3000}$

You can get the answer for **b** and **c** from your answer to **a**.

10 Convert each recurring decimal to a fraction.
   a $0.\dot{8}$ **b** $0.\dot{7}$ **c** $0.0\dot{5}$
   d 0.45 45 45…   **e** $0.\dot{6}\dot{3}$ **f** 0.038 383 8…
   g $0.00\dot{3}$ **h** $0.\dot{2}1\dot{6}$ **i** $0.0\dot{1}\dot{8}$
   j 0.756 756 756…   **k** $1.\dot{4}$ **l** $2.1\dot{4}$

Summary of key points

- The decimal point divides the units from the tenths.
- You can add and subtract decimals by writing them in columns. Make sure that the decimal points are in line.
- You can multiply or divide decimals by 10, 100, … by moving the digits 1, 2, … places to the left or right.
- You can divide a decimal by a whole number using the same method you use for whole numbers.
- A fraction can be converted to a decimal by dividing the numerator by the denominator.
- A decimal can be converted to a fraction by writing it as a number of tenths, hundredths, thousandths, …
- $\frac{1}{2} = 0.5$, $\frac{1}{4} = 0.25$, $\frac{3}{4} = 0.75$ and $\frac{1}{8} = 0.125$.
- When you multiply decimals, the sum of the decimal places in the numbers that are being multiplied gives the number of decimal places in the answer.
- To divide by a decimal, multiply both numbers to make the divisor a whole number.
- Fractions that have a combination of 2s and 5s as factors of the denominator convert to exact decimals. Other fractions give recurring decimals.
- A recurring decimal can be converted into a fraction by writing it as a product of the recurring digits and 0.111…, 0.0101…, 0.001 001…

Most candidates who get GRADE C or above can:
- add, subtract, multiply and divide decimals without a calculator.

Most candidates who get GRADE A or above can also:
- convert recurring decimals to fractions.

Glossary

Decimal place	a digit to the right of the decimal point
Denominator	the bottom number of a fraction
Fraction	part of a whole
Numerator	thc top number of a fraction
Place value	the position of a digit in a number that shows its value
Perimeter	the length of the lines enclosing a shape
Product	the result of multiplying two quantities together
Quadrilateral	a shape bounded by four straight lines
Recurring decimal	a decimal that goes on for ever with a repeating pattern of digits
Rounding	writing a number correct to a particular place value

5 Approximation and estimation

5.1 Significant figures

Peter measured the thickness of a book.
He wrote down 0.0205 metres.

Jane measured the same book.
She wrote down 20.5 millimetres.

The measurements are the same but they look different. This is because the units are different.

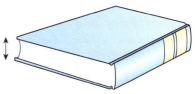

2.05 cm is also the same length.

The important, or significant, figures are the 2 and the 0 and 5 that follow it.
The 2 is the highest **place value** non-zero figure in both numbers. It is called the first **significant figure**.

Reading left to right the first significant figure in a number is the first non-zero digit, the second significant figure is the next digit and so on.

Example 1

a Write down the first significant figure and its value in the number 450.

b Write down the third significant figure and its value in the number 0.702.

    a 4. This figure is in the hundreds position, so its value is 400.

    b 2. This figure is in the third **decimal place** so its value is 2 thousandths.

Rounding to a given number of significant figures

To give a number correct to a number of significant figures, draw a
line after that significant figure and look at the digit after the line.
If this figure is less than 5, round down.
If this figure is 5 or more, round up.

Example 2

Write **a** 0.0635 correct to 2 significant figures
    b 7.773 correct to 3 significant figures
    c 34.507 correct to 4 significant figures
    d 19 ÷ 11 correct to 3 significant figures.

a 0.063|5 = 0.064 correct to 2 s.f.

> s.f. is an abbreviation
> for significant figures.

This is the 2nd s.f.

b 7.77|3 = 7.77 correct to 3 s.f.

This is the 3rd s.f.

c 34.50|7 = 34.51 correct to 4 s.f.

This is the 4th s.f.

d
$$\begin{array}{r} 1.72\,72 \\ 11\overline{)19.0000} \end{array}$$

19 ÷ 11 = 1.73 correct to 3 s.f.

> To give an answer correct to
> 3 s.f. you need to know the
> fourth significant figure.

Exam practice 5A

1 Write down the first significant figure in each number
and give its value.
  a 43   **b** 9.2   **c** 255   **d** 0.82
  e 0.065   **f** 24.88   **g** 20.03   **h** 502.2

2 Write down the third significant figure in each number and give
its value.
  a 70.6   **b** 0.04484   **c** 2.003
  d 26.7   **e** 107. 6   **f** 0.05052

3 Round each number to one significant figure.
  a 25.8   **b** 0.57   **c** 7967   **d** 580
  e 1.8   **f** 5.2   **g** 0.078   **h** 45.3

4 Give each number correct to the number of significant figures given in the brackets.
  a 36.3 (1 s.f.)   b 468.5 (3 s.f.)   c 0.0567 (2 s.f.)
  d 46.06 (3 s.f.)   e 0.05603 (3 s.f.)   f 88.807 (4 s.f.)
  g 3.073 (3 s.f.)   h 3.5087 (4 s.f.)

5 Give these numbers correct to 2 significant figures.
  a 2693   b 37 251   c 67 600   d 72 505
  e 9943   f 586   g 888   h 999

6 Give these numbers correct to 3 significant figures.
  a 64.88   b 0.07643   c 0.006438   d 354.77
  e 4.874   f 0.3762   g 10.555   h 0.004 6748

7 Find correct to 2 significant figures:
  a 10 ÷ 6   b 75 ÷ 9   c 0.44 ÷ 7   d 147 ÷ 8

> You need to continue the division until you have 3 significant figures.

8 Round each number to the accuracy given in brackets.
  a 3.572 (nearest unit)   b 0.0476 (3 d.p.)
  c 3994 (nearest 100)   d 0.00057 (1 s.f.)
  e 7.0478 (3 s.f.)   f 5.575 (2 d.p.)

9 Write each number correct to 1 significant figure.
  In each case state whether the rounded number is larger or smaller than the original number.
  a 53.978   b 0.0078547
  c 46.93106   d 0.00984503

10 Write each number correct to 3 significant figures.
  In each case state whether the corrected number has been rounded up or rounded down.
  a 52.55   b 0.04091   c 1.207   d 0.0002219

11 a Bella gave her weight as 51.2 kg correct to 1 decimal place.
      To how many significant figures did she round her weight?
  b Greg gave his height as 165 cm correct to the nearest centimetre.
      To how many significant figures did he round his height?

A01 12 Martin said that he took 30 minutes, to the nearest minute, to get to school this morning.
    Jana said 'That means you have rounded the time to 1 significant figure.'
    Is Jana correct? Give a reason for your answer.

> 'Give a reason' means write down why you answered yes or no.

A01 13 Don gave the width of a table as 120 cm correct to 2 significant figures.
    Mary asked if that was to the nearest centimetre.
    Write down, with a reason, what Don should tell Mary.

14 Find the value, correct to 3 significant figures, of:

   a $0.7 \div 3$ **b** $0.23 \div 9$ **c** $0.0013 \div 7$ **d** $\frac{14}{9}$

15 A stack of 6 concrete posts weighs 275 kg.
Find the weight of 1 post, giving your answer correct to
2 significant figures.

5.2 Estimating answers to calculations

Estimating the value of a calculation gives you an **approximate** answer.
Rounding the numbers to 1 significant figure will usually give a reasonable **estimate** that you can calculate in your head.

> You do not usually need an estimate to be as close as possible to the correct value. What you need to know is whether your calculation answer is the right order of size. A reasonable estimate will tell you that 69×52 is about 3500 not 350 or $35\,000$.

Example 3

Estimate the value of:

  a $21.2 \div 2.87$ **b** $6.871 \div 0.49$

  a $2|1.2 \div 2|.87 \approx 20 \div 3 \approx 6.6 = 7$ to 1 s.f.

> Round each number to one significant figure.
> Round your answer to 1 s.f.

  b $6.871 \div 0.49 \approx 7 \div 0.5 = 70 \div 5 = 14 \approx 10$ to 1 s.f.

You can get a better estimate by rounding some numbers to 2 significant figures.

> If the second significant figure in a number is 4, 5 or 6, you should round that number to 2 s.f.

Example 4

Estimate the value of 4.48×0.197.

  $4.48 \times 0.197 \approx 4.5 \times 0.2 = 0.9$

> Round the first number to 2 significant figures and the second number to 1 significant figure.

Exam practice 5B

1 Estimate the value of:

  a 15.6×12.13 **b** $596 \div 9.12$ **c** 31.6×8.3

  d $97.5 \div 4.8$ **e** $876 \div 241$ **f** $31.6 \div 8.3$

  g 577×21.5 **h** $294.4 + 149.77$ **i** $156 + 3904$

  j 0.37×0.14 **k** 0.43×0.27 **l** 4.49×0.75

2 Find an estimate for

  a $(4.9)^2$ **b** $(0.037)^2$ **c** $(0.294)^3$

  d $\frac{2.96}{3.94}$ **e** $\frac{8.33}{0.029}$ **f** $\frac{0.0688}{0.47}$

  g $0.39 \div 0.14$ **h** $1.37 \div 0.046$ **i** $\frac{0.0874}{0.0048}$

> Remember that $(4.9)^2$ means 4.9×4.9 and that $(0.294)^3$ means $0.294 \times 0.294 \times 0.294$.

3 Fayed bought 310 boxes of paper for his office.
Each box cost £9.56.
Estimate the total cost of the 310 boxes.

4 The answers given to these calculations are all wrong.
Decide whether each answer is too big or too small.
  a $278 \div 37 = 751$ b $72 + 85 = 83$ c $5.62 \times 1.15 = 4.16$
  d $\dfrac{3 + 6}{0.895} = 8.2$ e $\dfrac{3.84}{7.2 - 3.1} = 7.6$ f $(1.7)^2 = 4.1$

5 For each calculation, one of the answers given is correct. Use
estimation to find the correct answer.
  a 2.09×15.26 **A** 3.189 **B** 31.8934 **C** 45.72 **D** 0.0663
  b $(2.09)^2$ **A** 0.43681 **B** 437 **C** 25.9 **D** 4.3681
  c $\dfrac{32.2}{2.7}$ **A** 11.9$\dot{2}\dot{5}$ **B** 0.11$\dot{9}2\dot{5}$ **C** 166.1 **D** 0.01$\dot{6}$
  d $25 \times 42 \times 34$ **A** 357 **B** 35700 **C** 35.7 **D** 357 000

6 Find an approximate value of:
  a $\dfrac{32 \times 215}{56}$ b $\dfrac{(46.5 - 8.2)}{6.01}$
  c $\dfrac{3.11 \times 5.62^2}{43.7 + 21.2}$ d $\dfrac{4945 + 6012}{(1.7 - 0.5) \times 300}$

7 Estimate the value of:
  a $\dfrac{1.98^3}{41.7}$ b $\dfrac{71.9}{0.62^2 \times 1.36^2}$ c $\dfrac{25.2^2 - 9.8^2}{37 \times 20.9}$

8 The area of this shape is $\dfrac{3.142 \times (0.4106)^2}{3.44}$ cm².

Estimate this area.

9 £1837 was put into a savings account 2 years ago.
The amount now in the account is
£1837 × 1.0425 × 1.047.
  a Estimate the amount in
     the account.
  b Is your estimate more
     or less than the actual
     amount?
     Explain your answer.

> • When you round a number up,
>   multiplying by or adding that number produces an overestimate,
>   dividing by or subtracting that number produces an underestimate.
> • When you round a number down,
>   multiplying by or adding that number produces an underestimate,
>   dividing by or subtracting that number produces an overestimate.

10 The number of puffins on Ase Island is approximately 27 000.
The number is expected to increase to 27 000 × 1.8 next year.
  a Estimate the number of puffins next year.
  b In three years' time the number is expected to be 27 000 × 1.8³.
     Estimate the number of puffins in three years' time.
     How accurate do you think your estimate is?

11 David used his calculator to find 2.13 + 9.32 × 0.21.
He wrote down the answer as 2.08 correct to 2 decimal places.
Explain how you know that David's answer is wrong.

12 Which of these estimates is nearest to the value of $\dfrac{1.18 \times 0.78}{1.37^2}$?

   A $\dfrac{1 \times 0.8}{1}$ **B** $\dfrac{1 \times 1}{1}$ **C** $\dfrac{1 \times 0.8}{2}$

5.3 Estimating square roots

When you estimate the square root of a number, these facts will help
you to check your answer.
- The square root of a number bigger than 1 is smaller than the
  number.
- The square root of a number smaller than 1 is larger than the
  number.

$\sqrt{225} = 15$ and
$\sqrt{0.16} = 0.4$.

Example 5

Estimate the square root of: **a** 376   **b** 2735

a $\sqrt{\overline{3}\,\overline{76}} \simeq \sqrt{\overline{4}\,\overline{00}} = 20$

Start by grouping the digits in pairs from the
decimal point.
Each group gives one digit in the answer.

Round the left-hand
group to the nearest
square number. Replace
all other digits with zero.

There are two groups.
This means there are
two digits in the square
root.

b $\sqrt{\overline{27}\,\overline{35}} \simeq \sqrt{\overline{25}\,\overline{00}} = 50$

The nearest square number to 27 is 25.

Example 6

Estimate the square root of:
a 0.08657   **b** 0.00567

a $\sqrt{0.\overline{08}\,\overline{657}} \simeq \sqrt{0.\overline{09}} = 0.3$

Group in pairs after the decimal point until you
have included at least one digit that is not 0.

There is no need to put
zeros here because you
only want one decimal
place.

b $\sqrt{0.\overline{00}\,\overline{576}} \simeq \sqrt{0.\overline{00}\,\overline{64}} = 0.08$

The first group after the point is 00. This gives 0 in the
first decimal place of the square root. The next pair, 64,
gives 8 in the second decimal place in the square root.

Exam practice 5C

1. Estimate the positive square root of:
   - a   94   b   576   c   4683   d   7967   e   11 788

   > Square your answer to check that it makes sense.

2. Estimate:
   - a $\sqrt{0.6375}$ b $\sqrt{0.8464}$ c $\sqrt{0.0145}$ d $\sqrt{0.0024}$

3. Estimate the value of:
   - a $\sqrt{0.0957}$ b $\sqrt{0.06342}$ c $\sqrt{0.003756}$
   - d $\sqrt{0.008734}$ e $\sqrt{0.000264}$ f $\sqrt{0.0000463}$

4. Estimate the value of:
   - a $\sqrt{29}$ b $\sqrt{110}$ c $\dfrac{1}{\sqrt{13}}$ d $\sqrt{6325}$

5. Estimate the value of
   - a $\sqrt{(6.45^2 - 9.46)}$ b $\sqrt{\dfrac{2.56}{0.133}}$ c $\sqrt{\dfrac{56004}{2.67^2}}$

5.4 Using a calculator

Most questions will tell you how to round your answer; for example, to 3 significant figures or 2 decimal places or to the nearest 10. This is called the **degree of accuracy.**

When you use your calculator, you will often find that there are many more digits in the display than you need. You do not have to write all these figures down. Write down one more digit than you need for your answer.

Example 7

Use you calculator to find $\dfrac{1.75 + 0.924}{2.477}$ correct to 3 significant figures.

$$\frac{1.75 + 0.924}{2.477} = 1.07|9\ldots$$
$$= 1.08 \text{ correct to 3 s.f.}$$

> Use brackets around 1.75 + 0.924 so that the calculator does this first: press
> (1 . 7 5 + 0 . 9 2 4)
> ÷ 2 . 4 7 7 =
> The display shows 1.079531692.
> To give this correct to 3 s.f., write down the first 4 significant figures.

If you do your working in more than one step on your calculator, use the memory to store answers you will need again. If you have an answer key, you can enter the answer to the last calculation.

Example 8

Find $\dfrac{5.88}{1.22 \times 12.9}$ correct to 3 decimal places.

$\dfrac{5.88}{1.22 \times 12.9} = 0.3736\ldots$

$= 0.374$ correct to 3 decimal places.

Work out the bottom first: ①.②②×①②.⑨:
the display shows 15.738. Then enter ⑤.⑧⑧÷ANS=:
this gives 0.3736...
You could also use brackets to do the calculation in one step: press
⑤.⑧⑧÷(①.②②×①②.⑨)=.

Choosing an appropriate degree of accuracy

When an answer is not exact, you may be told how accurate your answer should be. Sometimes you have to decide yourself.

When a calculation involves exact values, round your answer to 3 significant figures.

For calculations where the values could have been rounded, give your answers to the same degree of accuracy as the values given. In the calculation 523×0.24 kg, you can see that 0.24 kg is rounded to 2 significant figures, so you should give your answer correct to 2 significant figures.

Continuous quantities such as length are always rounded. If values are given to different numbers of significant figures, choose the least number for your answer.

When the calculation involves money, it is sensible to give answers correct to the nearest penny.

Class discussion

What degree of accuracy is appropriate in these situations?
- Jane is going to drive from London to Manchester. She wants to know how far it is.
- Razia needs to give her height in metres for a passport application.
- Johannes wants to know if a tall bookcase will fit in his living room.
- Karl wants to know the amount of interest on £2500 in a savings account.

When you are asked to give an exact answer for a calculation involving numbers such as π or $\sqrt{2}$ you must leave them in your answer.

The exact value of $8\pi \div 4$ is 2π.

Exam practice 5D

1 Use your calculator to find, correct to 3 significant figures, the value of:

    a 33.8×4.601 b $50.3 \div 3.74$

    c $500 \div 38.7$ d $6711 \div 159.2$

First make an estimate. This will tell you whether your calculator answer is the right sort of size.

2 Find, correct to 3 significant figures, the value of:

    a 34.2×30.7 b 5007×2.51

    c $0.279 \div 0.521$ d 36.8×41.5

    e $0.476 - 0.35 \times 0.53$ f $0.0226 \times 0.352 + 0.038$

    g $6.844 + 1.36 \div 0.007\,46$ h $64.4 \times (32.05 - 9.49)$

    i $5.08 \div (1.855 - 0.894)$ j $0.44 \div (0.44 + 0.366)$

Remember that you do multiplication and division before addition and subtraction.

3 Find, correct to 3 significant figures, the value of:

a $\dfrac{0.057}{2.22 + 0.9317}$ b $\dfrac{5.788 - 2.911}{0.878}$ c $\dfrac{0.58}{0.067 \times 1.44}$

d $\dfrac{294}{21.5^2}$ e $\dfrac{38.2^2}{127}$ f $\dfrac{0.194 - 0.087}{0.102}$

g $\dfrac{25.7 - 18.8}{26.5 + 5.3}$ h $\dfrac{29.304 + 18.37}{189.3}$

> Use brackets when necessary.
>
> To find 21.5^2 on a calculator, press
> 2 1 . 5 x^2 = .

4 Calculate the value of:

a $\dfrac{2.5}{1.8 \times 0.77}$ b $\dfrac{4.55 + 3.32}{2.79}$

c $\dfrac{0.51 + 1.7}{0.095}$ d $\dfrac{1.3^3}{2.6}$

Give your answers correct to 3 significant figures.

> To find 1.3^3 on a calculator, press
> 1 . 3 x^y 3 = .

5 Find, correct to 3 significant figures.

a $\sqrt{12}$ b $\sqrt{54}$ c $\sqrt{120}$

> To find a square root, press the $\sqrt{\ }$ key, then enter the number and press = .

6 Find correct to 3 significant figures.

a $\sqrt[3]{20}$ b $\sqrt[3]{100}$ c $\dfrac{1}{\sqrt[3]{5}}$

> Find out how to find cube roots on your calculator.

A01 7 Hillary estimated 2.49×1.49 as roughly 2.

a Calculate 2.49×1.49.

b Find the difference between your answer and Hillary's estimate.

c How can Hillary could improve the accuracy of her estimate.

8 Plant cells are grown in a laboratory.
When conditions are perfect, the number of cells after 3 hours is $25 \times (1.05)^3$.
Work out the number of cells. Give your answer to a suitable degree of accuracy.

A01 9 Andy worked out that he can get 375 cups of coffee from a 250 g jar of instant coffee powder using 1.2 grams of powder per cup.

a Explain how you know that he is wrong.

b Find the number of cups that Andy can get.

10 John measured the length of a floor as 5.25 metres and its width as 3.67 metres.
The cost of varnishing the floor is $£5.25 \times 3.67 \times 1.99$.
Find the cost, giving your answer to a suitable degree of accuracy.
Write down the degree of accuracy you have chosen and why you chose it.

11 a Round each number in $\dfrac{1.27}{1.23 - 0.97}$ to 1 significant figure.

b Explain why you cannot use these numbers to find an estimate for $\dfrac{1.27}{1.23 - 0.97}$.

c Find an approximate value for $\dfrac{1.27}{1.23 - 0.97}$. Show your working.

d Calculate the value of $\dfrac{1.27}{1.23 - 0.97}$.

Summary of key points

- The first significant figure in a number is the first non-zero digit. The second significant figure is the next digit to the right, and so on.
- To round to a given number of significant figures, look at the next digit to the right. If it is 5 or more, round up, otherwise round down.
- You can usually find an approximate value of a calculation by rounding each number to 1 significant figure.
- When the second significant figure is 4, 5 or 6, rounding the number to 2 significant figures will give a better estimate, provided it does not make the calculation too hard.
- You can estimate the value of a square root by grouping the numbers in pairs from the decimal point.

Most candidates who get GRADE C or above can:
- estimate answers to calculations.

Most candidates who get GRADE A or above can also:
- decide on a suitable degree of accuracy for an answer.

Glossary

Approximation	a rough value
Decimal place	the position of a digit after the decimal point
Degree of accuracy	the place value or significant figure to which a number is rounded
Estimate	a rough value
Place value	the position of a digit in a number that shows its value
Rounding	writing a number to a given degree of accuracy
Significant figure	the first significant figure of a number is the first non-zero digit and the second significant figure is the next digit to the right, and so on

6 Indices and standard form

This chapter will show you:
- ✓ how to multiply and divide numbers written in index form
- ✓ the meaning of a^1 and a^0
- ✓ what a negative index means
- ✓ the meaning of fractional indices and how to work with them
- ✓ the laws of indices
- ✓ what a surd is and how to rationalise an expression which has a surd in the denominator
- ✓ the meaning of standard form
- ✓ how to add, subtract, multiply and divide numbers in standard form
- ✓ how to use a calculator when working with numbers in standard form

Before you start you need to know:
- ✓ the meaning of indices
- ✓ how to add, subtract, multiply and divide decimals
- ✓ how to work with negative numbers
- ✓ the meaning of significant figures
- ✓ the meaning of reciprocal

6.1 Multiplying and dividing numbers written in index form

You can multiply the *same* number with different **powers** by adding the powers.

$$2^3 \times 2^2 = (2 \times 2 \times 2) \times (2 \times 2) = 2^5 = 2^{3+2}$$

You can divide the *same* number with different powers by subtracting the powers.

$$3^5 \div 3^3 = \frac{\cancel{3} \times \cancel{3} \times \cancel{3} \times 3 \times 3}{\cancel{3} \times \cancel{3} \times \cancel{3}} = 3 \times 3 = 3^2 = 3^{5-3}$$

Example 1

Simplify: **a** $2^5 \times 2^2$ **b** $2^5 \div 2^2$

$$2^5 \times 2^2 = 2^{5+2} = 2^7$$

> You are multiplying so add the powers.

$$2^5 \div 2^2 = 2^{5-2} = 2^3$$

> You are dividing so subtract the powers.

You cannot use the rules when the base numbers are different.
This means that you can not simplify $5^3 \times 3^2$ or $5^3 \div 3^2$.

Numbers to the power zero

$2^3 \div 2^3 = 2^{3-3} = 2^0$

A number divided by itself equals 1, so $2^3 \div 2^3 = 1$.
This means that $2^0 = 1$.

Any number to the power zero is 1.

Exam practice 6A

1 Simplify:

a $3^5 \times 3^3$	b $7^5 \times 7^2$	c $9^3 \times 9^7$	d $2^3 \times 2^6$
e $4^7 \times 4^9$	f $5^4 \times 5^4$	g $12^4 \times 12^5$	h $6^6 \times 6^3$

> These are multiplications so add the powers.

 2 Graham said that $10^4 \times 10^3 = 10^{12}$.
Is Graham correct? Give a reason for your answer.

 3 Holly said that $10^9 \times 10^8 = 10^{17}$.
Is Holly correct? Give a reason for your answer.

4 Simplify:

a $7^4 \div 7^2$	b $2^7 \div 2^5$	c $5^6 \div 5^5$	d $3^7 \div 3^4$
e $2^8 \div 2^6$	f $5^5 \div 5^4$	g $3^4 \div 3$	h $5^9 \div 5$

> These are divisions so subtract the powers.

> $3 = 3^1$

5 Kim said that $7^9 \div 7^3 = 7^3$.
Kim is wrong. Explain her mistake.

6 Simplify:

a $3^5 \div 3^5$	b $4^7 \div 4^6$	c $a^6 \div a^5$	d $x^2 \times x^3$
e $m^2 \times m^2$	f $b^9 \div b^6$	g $x^{10} \div x^{10}$	h $p^{11} \times p^3$

> The letters represent numbers.

7 a Write $(2^4)^3$ as a single power of 2.

   b Write $(5^2)^5$ as a single power of 5.

   c Write $(0.3^3)^3$ as a single power of 0.3.

> $(2^4)^3 = 2^4 \times 2^4 \times 2^4$

8 Find the value of:

a $3^3 \div 3^3$	b $4^3 \div 4^2$	c $7^3 \times 7^2 \div 7^5$
d $4^2 \times 4^0$	e $5^3 \times 5^0 \div 5^1$	f $a^3 \times a^5 \div a^0$

9 Jim said '$4^0 \div 2^4 = 2^2$'. Is he right? Explain your answer.

6.2 Negative indices

When dividing numbers in **index** form, you sometimes get a negative index.

$$2^3 \div 2^5 = 2^{3-5} = 2^{-2} \text{ and } 2^3 \div 2^5 = \frac{2^3}{2^5} = \frac{2 \times 2 \times 2}{2 \times 2 \times 2 \times 2 \times 2} = \frac{1}{2^2}$$

So $2^{-2} = \dfrac{1}{2^2}$

> $\dfrac{1}{2^2}$ is the reciprocal of 2^2.

A negative sign in the index means 'the *reciprocal* of'.

Example 2

Express 5^{-3} as a fraction.

$$5^{-3} = \frac{1}{5^3} = \frac{1}{5 \times 5 \times 5} = \frac{1}{125}$$

5^{-3} means the reciprocal of 5^3.

Laws of indices

You can write the laws of indices using letters to represent any number:

1 $a^x \times a^y = a^{x+y}$

2 $a^x \div a^y = a^{x-y}$

3 $a^{-x} = \left(\frac{1}{a}\right)^x$

Exam practice 6B

1 Find the value of:
   a 2^{-3} b 3^{-2} c 2^{-4} d 10^{-2} e 3^{-1} f 5^{-3}

2 Write these numbers as fractions.
   a 10^{-3} b 10^{-5} c 10^{-4} d 10^{-1}

3 Write these numbers as decimals.
   a 10^{-4} b 10^{-2} c 10^{-3} d 10^{-6}

4 Simplify:
   a $3^4 \times 3^{-2}$ b $4^{-3} \times 4^2$ c $2^{-2} \times 2^{-5}$
   d $4^4 \times 4^{-1}$ e $2^{-3} \times 2^5$ f $3^{-2} \times 3^{-3}$
   g $3^4 \div 3^6$ h $2^7 \div 2^9$ i $3^{-2} \div 3^7$
   j $3^4 \div 3^{-2}$ k $5^{-2} \div 5^{-6}$ l $2^{-4} \div 2^{-7}$

> Add the indices when multiplying the same base numbers.
> Subtract the indices when dividing the same base numbers.
> Subtracting a negative number is the same as adding a positive number
> so $3^7 \div 3^{-4} = 3^{7-(-4)}$
> $= 3^{7+4}$.

5 Find the value of:
   a $2^3 \times 3^{-2}$ b $5^{-2} \times 2^3$ c $2^{-5} \times 3^{-4}$
   d $5^2 \div 2^2$ e $3^{-2} \div 2^3$ f $4^3 \div 2^5$

> Find the value of each number, then multiply them.

6 Write these numbers using negative indices.
   a $\frac{1}{5^2}$ b $\frac{1}{2^4}$ c $\frac{1}{10^2}$ d $\frac{1}{7^3}$ e $\frac{1}{5^5}$ f $\frac{1}{10^{12}}$

7 Write these numbers as powers of 10.
   a 10 b 1 c $\frac{1}{10}$ d $\frac{1}{100}$ e $\frac{1}{1000}$ f $\frac{1}{1\,000\,000}$

> $\frac{1}{100} = \frac{1}{10^2} = 10^{-2}$

8 Find the value of:
   a $2^{-1} \times 2^0$ b $3^0 \div 4^2$ c $5^3 \times 5^{-2}$

> Any number to the power 1 is equal to itself.

9 Work out the value of:
   a $2^4 \div 2^6 \times 2^0$ b $5^3 \times 5^{-2} \div 5^5$ c $4^2 \times 4^{-7} \div (2^2)^{-7}$
   d $\frac{3^3 \times 3^4}{3^5}$ e $\frac{5^3}{5^2 \times 5^0}$ f $\left(\frac{1}{2}\right)^{-1}$
   g $\left(\frac{2}{3}\right)^{-2}$ h $\left(\frac{1}{4}\right)^2 \times \left(\frac{1}{2}\right)^{-3}$ i $\left(\frac{2}{3}\right)^2 \times \left(\frac{3}{4}\right)^{-2}$

> $\left(\frac{1}{2}\right)^{-1}$ means the reciprocal of $\frac{1}{2}$.

6.3 Fractional indices

An index can be a fraction:
$$\left(2^{\frac{1}{2}}\right)^2 = 2^{\frac{1}{2}} \times 2^{\frac{1}{2}} = 2^1 = 2.$$
So $2^{\frac{1}{2}}$ means $\sqrt{2}$.

> When a number is squared, the starting number is the square root of the result.

$$\left(8^{\frac{1}{3}}\right)^3 = 8^{\frac{1}{3}} \times 8^{\frac{1}{3}} \times 8^{\frac{1}{3}} = 8^{\frac{1}{3}+\frac{1}{3}+\frac{1}{3}} = 8^1 = 8.$$
So $8^{\frac{1}{3}}$ means $\sqrt[3]{8}$.

> When a number is cubed, the starting number is the cube root of the result.

An index of $\frac{1}{n}$ means the nth root of the base number.

Example 3

Find: **a** $\left(\dfrac{1}{64}\right)^{\frac{1}{2}}$ **b** $(0.36)^{\frac{1}{2}}$ **c** $\left(\dfrac{27}{8}\right)^{\frac{1}{3}}$

a $\left(\dfrac{1}{64}\right)^{\frac{1}{2}} = \sqrt{\dfrac{1}{64}} = \dfrac{1}{8}$

b $(0.36)^{\frac{1}{2}} = \sqrt{0.36} = 0.6$

c $\left(\dfrac{27}{8}\right)^{\frac{1}{3}} = \sqrt[3]{\dfrac{27}{8}} = \dfrac{3}{2}$

> $\sqrt[3]{\dfrac{27}{8}} = \dfrac{\sqrt[3]{27}}{\sqrt[3]{8}}$

Powers of powers

When you raise a power to a power you multiply the indices.
$$(2^3)^4 = 2^3 \times 2^3 \times 2^3 \times 2^3 = 2^{3 \times 4}$$

The general rule is $(a^x)^y = a^{xy}$.

You can use this rule to find fractional powers.
$$8^{\frac{2}{3}} = 8^{\frac{1}{3} \times 2} = \left(8^{\frac{1}{3}}\right)^2 = 2^2 = 4$$

Example 4

Find: **a** $\left(\dfrac{16}{81}\right)^{\frac{3}{4}}$ **b** $(0.001)^{-\frac{2}{3}}$

a $\left(\dfrac{16}{81}\right)^{\frac{3}{4}} = \left(\left(\dfrac{16}{81}\right)^{\frac{1}{4}}\right)^3 = \left(\dfrac{2}{3}\right)^3 = \dfrac{8}{27}$

> $2 \times 2 \times 2 \times 2 = 16$ and $3 \times 3 \times 3 \times 3 = 81$

b $(0.001)^{-\frac{2}{3}} = (1000)^{\frac{2}{3}} = (1000^{\frac{1}{3}})^2 = 10^2 = 100$

> The negative index means the reciprocal.

Exam practice 6C

Find the value of:

1 a $4^{\frac{1}{2}}$ b $9^{\frac{1}{2}}$ c $16^{\frac{1}{2}}$ d $36^{\frac{1}{2}}$

   e $27^{\frac{1}{3}}$ f $64^{\frac{1}{3}}$ g $125^{\frac{1}{3}}$ h $216^{\frac{1}{3}}$

   i $4^{-\frac{1}{2}}$ j $729^{-\frac{1}{3}}$ k $100^{-\frac{1}{2}}$ l $81^{-\frac{1}{4}}$

> $4^{-\frac{1}{2}}$ means the reciprocal of $4^{\frac{1}{2}}$.

2 a $\left(\frac{1}{4}\right)^{\frac{1}{2}}$ b $\left(\frac{1}{36}\right)^{\frac{1}{2}}$ c $\left(\frac{4}{25}\right)^{\frac{1}{2}}$ d $\left(\frac{9}{64}\right)^{\frac{1}{2}}$

   e $(0.01)^{\frac{1}{2}}$ f $(0.25)^{\frac{1}{2}}$ g $(0.04)^{\frac{1}{2}}$ h $(0.81)^{\frac{1}{2}}$

3 a $\left(\frac{1}{8}\right)^{\frac{1}{3}}$ b $\left(\frac{8}{27}\right)^{\frac{1}{3}}$ c $\left(\frac{125}{64}\right)^{\frac{1}{3}}$ d $\left(3\frac{3}{8}\right)^{\frac{1}{3}}$

   e $\left(\frac{1}{4}\right)^{-\frac{1}{2}}$ f $\left(\frac{1}{125}\right)^{-\frac{1}{3}}$ g $\left(2\frac{1}{4}\right)^{-\frac{1}{2}}$ h $0.01^{-\frac{1}{2}}$

4 a $4^{\frac{3}{2}}$ b $27^{\frac{2}{3}}$ c $25^{\frac{3}{2}}$ d $125^{\frac{2}{3}}$

   e $(0.008)^{\frac{2}{3}}$ f $(0.36)^{\frac{3}{2}}$ g $1000^{\frac{2}{3}}$ h $81^{\frac{3}{4}}$

5 a $64^{\frac{2}{3}}$ b $144^{\frac{3}{2}}$ c $8^{\frac{4}{3}}$ d $0.027^{\frac{2}{3}}$

   e $\left(\frac{8}{27}\right)^{\frac{2}{3}}$ f $\left(\frac{8}{125}\right)^{\frac{2}{3}}$ g $\left(\frac{1}{1000}\right)^{\frac{2}{3}}$ h $\left(\frac{4}{25}\right)^{\frac{5}{2}}$

6.4 Surds

Any number that can be written in the form $\frac{a}{b}$ where a and b are integers and $b \neq 0$ is called a **rational number**.

> $\frac{22}{7}$, -8 and $\sqrt{9}$ are rational numbers.

Numbers that cannot be written in this way are called **irrational numbers**. They cannot be written as an exact or recurring decimal.

$\sqrt{2}$, $\sqrt{3}$, are called **surds**.

> $\sqrt{2}$, $\sqrt{3}$ and π are irrational numbers.

When an answer is irrational you can give the exact value by using surds or π in your answer.

You can simplify surds using this rule: $\sqrt{a \times b} = \sqrt{a} \times \sqrt{b}$

Example 5

Simplify the following giving your answers exactly, in surd form where necessary.

a $\sqrt{50}$ b $(\sqrt{3})^2$ c $\sqrt{18} \times \sqrt{2}$

a $\sqrt{50} = \sqrt{25 \times 2} = \sqrt{25} \times \sqrt{2} = 5 \times \sqrt{2} = 5\sqrt{2}$

> You cannot simplify $5\sqrt{2}$ any more.

b $(\sqrt{3})^2 = \sqrt{3} \times \sqrt{3} = \sqrt{9} = 3$

c $\sqrt{18} \times \sqrt{2} = \sqrt{36} = 6$

Rationalising the denominator

If an expression has a surd in the denominator, you can multiply the top and bottom of the fraction by that surd. This turns the denominator into a rational number. It is called 'rationalising the denominator'.

Example 6

Rationalise the denominator of: **a** $\dfrac{3}{\sqrt{18}}$ **b** $\dfrac{2\sqrt{5}}{5\sqrt{3}}$

a $\dfrac{3}{\sqrt{18}} = \dfrac{3}{\sqrt{9} \times \sqrt{2}} = \dfrac{3}{3 \times \sqrt{2}} = \dfrac{3 \times \sqrt{2}}{3 \times \sqrt{2} \times \sqrt{2}} = \dfrac{3\sqrt{2}}{3 \times 2} = \dfrac{\sqrt{2}}{2}$

> $3 \times \sqrt{2}$ is written as $3\sqrt{2}$.

> Multiply top and bottom by $\sqrt{2}$.

b $\dfrac{2\sqrt{5}}{5\sqrt{3}} = \dfrac{2\sqrt{5} \times \sqrt{3}}{5\sqrt{3} \times \sqrt{3}} = \dfrac{2\sqrt{5}\sqrt{3}}{5 \times 3} = \dfrac{2\sqrt{15}}{15}$

> Multiply top and bottom by $\sqrt{3}$.

Exam practice 6D

1 Simplify the following, giving your answers exactly using surds.

> In part **a**, start by writing 12 as 4×3.

   a $\sqrt{12}$ **b** $\sqrt{50}$ **c** $\sqrt{8}$ **d** $\sqrt{63}$

   e $\sqrt{200}$ **f** $\sqrt{48}$ **g** $\sqrt{72}$ **h** $\sqrt{28}$

2 Write each of the following as a whole number.

   a $\sqrt{2} \times \sqrt{8}$ **b** $\sqrt{2} \times \sqrt{72}$ **c** $(\sqrt{5})^2$ **d** $\sqrt{5} \times \sqrt{20}$

   e $\sqrt{3} \times \sqrt{12}$ **f** $\sqrt{2} \times \sqrt{32}$ **g** $(\sqrt{7})^2$ **h** $\sqrt{18} \times \sqrt{2}$

3 Rationalise the denominator and simplify:

   a $\dfrac{1}{\sqrt{3}}$ **b** $\dfrac{1}{\sqrt{5}}$ **c** $\dfrac{3}{\sqrt{3}}$ **d** $\dfrac{5}{\sqrt{5}}$ **e** $\dfrac{2}{\sqrt{10}}$

   f $\dfrac{7}{\sqrt{7}}$ **g** $\dfrac{14}{\sqrt{14}}$ **h** $\dfrac{\sqrt{2}}{\sqrt{3}}$ **i** $\dfrac{\sqrt{5}}{\sqrt{10}}$ **j** $\dfrac{4}{\sqrt{12}}$

4 Rationalise the denominator and simplify:

   a $\dfrac{\sqrt{6}}{3\sqrt{3}}$ **b** $\dfrac{\sqrt{50}}{5\sqrt{2}}$ **c** $\dfrac{3}{\sqrt{18}}$ **d** $\dfrac{\sqrt{2}}{\sqrt{50}}$ **e** $\dfrac{\sqrt{12}}{2\sqrt{3}}$

> You need to multiply both numbers on top by the surd.

5 Rationalise the denominator and simplify:

   a $\dfrac{(2 - \sqrt{2})}{\sqrt{2}}$ **b** $\dfrac{(2 + \sqrt{3})}{\sqrt{3}}$ **c** $\dfrac{(3 + 2\sqrt{3})}{\sqrt{3}}$ **d** $\dfrac{(3 + \sqrt{5})}{\sqrt{5}}$

> There is more work on surds in Chapter 9.

6.5 Standard form

It is difficult to compare the size of these two numbers because one is in billions and the other is in millions.

Very large numbers or very small numbers are easier to compare when they are written in the same notation.

The form that is used in science is called **standard form**.

A number written in standard form is a number between 1 and 10 multiplied by a power of 10.

CONSUMER CREDIT STANDS AT £52.6 BILLION

£50 MILLION BANK HEIST

> The numbers 1.3×10^2 and 3.72×10^{-3} are in standard form.
> The numbers 13×10^5 and 0.26×10^{-3} are not in standard form because the first number is not between 1 and 10.

Example 7

Write 5.976×10^{24} in full.

$$5.976 \times 10^{24} = 5\,976\,000\,000\,000\,000\,000\,000\,000.$$

> 5.976×10^{24} means 5.976 multiplied by ten 24 times. This means you have to move the digits 24 places to the left. Fill in the gaps with zeros.

Example 8

The time light takes to travel 1 km is $3.335\,609 \times 10^{-6}$ seconds.
Write the number in full.

$$3.335\,609 \times 10^{-6} = 3.335\,609 \times \frac{1}{10^6}$$
$$= 3.335\,609 \div 10^6$$
$$= 3.335\,609 \div 1\,000\,000$$
$$= 0.000\,003\,335\,609.$$

> $10^{-6} = \frac{1}{10^6}$. So
> $3.335\,609 \times 10^{-6}$ means $3.335\,609 \div 10^6$
> $= 3.335\,609 \div 1\,000\,000$.
> You have to move the digits 6 places to the right. Fill in the gaps with zeros.

Example 9

Write in standard form: **a**   6800   **b**   0.01934

a $6800 = 6.8 \times 1000$
$$= 6.8 \times 10^3$$

b $0.01934 = 1.934 \div 100$
$$= 1.934 \times \frac{1}{100}$$
$$= 1.934 \times 10^{-2}$$

> Place the decimal point between the 6 and the 8 to give a number between 1 and 10. This gives 6.8. You have to multiply 6.8 by 1000 to get 6800.

> The decimal point has to go between the 1 and the 9 to give a number between 1 and 10. You have to divide 1.934 by 100 to get 0.01934.

Exam practice 6E

1   Write these numbers in full.

   a 5.5×10^3 b 3.16×10^5 c 4.155×10^6

   d 5.778×10^2 e 1.3×10^4 f 9.15×10^3

   g 8.022×10^4 h 2.004×10^8 i 7.4×10^6

   j 2.04×10^7 k 7.402×10^3 l 3.101×10^{11}

2   Write these numbers in full.

   a 4.7×10^{-3} b 1.35×10^{-5} c 3.103×10^{-4}

   d 7.71×10^{-1} e 2.9×10^{-5} f 8.01×10^{-4}

   g 5.008×10^{-2} h 2.052×10^{-8} i 5.1×10^{-4}

   j 6.35×10^{-2} k 6.027×10^{-6} l 3.889×10^{-10}

3   Write these numbers in full.

   a 3.78×10^3 b 5.3×10^6 c 6.43×10^{-8}

   d 4.77×10^{-4} e 1.26×10^{-3} f 7.4×10^{14}

   g 4.25×10^{12} h 9.08×10^{-7}

4   Write the following numbers in standard form:

   a   2800   b   420   c   39 070

   d   76 040   e   4 500 000   f   547 000

   g   15 300   h   43 000 000   i   260 000

   j   40 000   k   5 091 000   l   704

> Place the decimal
> point between the first
> and second significant
> figure. Then decide
> what power of ten this
> needs to be multiplied
> by or divided by to
> make it equal to the
> original number.

5   Write the following numbers in standard form.

   a   0.036   b   0.77   c   0.707

   d   0.0084   e   0.035   f   0.0096

   g   0.0402   h   0.000 006 6   i   0.000 049

   j   0.000 000 007   k   0.000 602 2   l   0.08

6   Write the following numbers in standard form:

   a   0.684   b   0.000 000 000 073   c   0.0011

   d   0.0535   e   88.92   f   0.000 050 6

   g   0.000 000 057   h   503 000 000

7   The mass of the Earth is 5 976 000 000 000 000 000 000 000 kg.
    Write this mass in standard form.

8   The mass of the sun is
    1 900 000 000 000 000 000 000 000 000 000 kg.
    Write this mass in standard form.

9   A noise level of 10^{12} decibels is painful.
    Write this noise level in full.

10   The Earth is 150 million kilometres from the sun.
     Write this distance in standard form.

11 Bacteria are single living cells.
One cell has a diameter of about 7.08×10^{-5} cm.
Write this number in full.

12 Write each set of numbers in standard form.
Then place them in order of size, smallest first.
   a 576 000 000, 20 000 000 000, 997 000 000, 247 000, 37500
   b 0.00527, 0.60005, 0.9906, 0.000 000 050 2, 0.003 005
   c 0.0705, 7.08, 79.3, 0.007 008 09, 560 800.

13 When the number 1.225×10^{12} is written in full, how many
zeros are there after the 5?

14 Find $1\,200\,000 \times 40\,000$ and write your answer in standard
form.

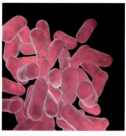

10^3 is larger than 10^2
and 10^{-3} is smaller
than 10^{-2}.

6.6 Working with numbers in standard form

When you multiply and divide numbers in standard form, you do
not need to write them in full.

Example 10

Work out the following, giving your answers in standard form.

a $(2.1 \times 10^8) \times (5 \times 10^6)$

b $\dfrac{2.1 \times 10^8}{5 \times 10^6}$

This is not in standard
form. To change it into
standard form write
10.5 as 1.05×10^1

You can change
the order in which
the numbers are
multiplied.

a $2.1 \times 10^8 \times 5 \times 10^6 = 2.1 \times 5 \times 10^8 \times 10^6$
$= 10.5 \times 10^{14}$
2.1 × 5
$= 1.05 \times 10^1 \times 10^{14}$ $10^8 \times 10^6 = 10^{8+6}$
$= 1.05 \times 10^{15}$

b $\dfrac{2.1 \times 10^8}{5 \times 10^6} = \dfrac{2.1}{5} \times \dfrac{10^8}{10^6}$
$= 0.42 \times 10^{8-6}$
$= 0.42 \times 10^2$
$= 4.2 \times 10^{-1} \times 10^2$
$= 4.2 \times 10^1$

When a calculation involves addition and subtraction, you must write out the numbers in full.

Example 11

Find $2.8 \times 10^4 + 1.7 \times 10^3$.

> If the numbers are given in standard form you should give your answers in standard form.

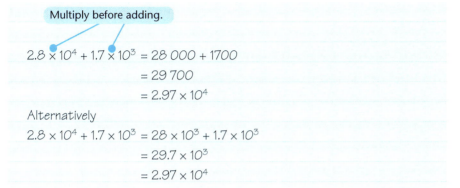

Multiply before adding.

$2.8 \times 10^4 + 1.7 \times 10^3 = 28\,000 + 1700$
$= 29\,700$
$= 2.97 \times 10^4$

Alternatively

$2.8 \times 10^4 + 1.7 \times 10^3 = 28 \times 10^3 + 1.7 \times 10^3$
$= 29.7 \times 10^3$
$= 2.97 \times 10^4$

Exam practice 6F

> Remember that numbers can be multiplied in any order. You can rearrange so that the powers of ten are next to each other. Remember also that you can multiply different powers of the same base number by adding the powers.

1 Work out the following, giving your answers in standard form:

a $2 \times 10^3 \times 3 \times 10^5$
b $2 \times 10^5 \times 4 \times 10^8$
c $3 \times 10^2 \times 7 \times 10^8$
d $8 \times 10^5 \times 2 \times 10^5$
e $2.1 \times 10^4 \times 4 \times 10^3$
f $5.4 \times 10^4 \times 2 \times 10^5$
g $1.6 \times 10^8 \times 5 \times 10^3$
h $3 \times 10^{10} \times 4.5 \times 10^3$

2 Find the following, giving your answers in standard form:

a $2 \times 10^6 \times 3 \times 10^{-4}$
b $6 \times 10^{-6} \times 3 \times 10^{12}$
c $6 \times 10^{-8} \times 5 \times 10^5$
d $1.5 \times 10^4 \times 4 \times 10^{-2}$
e $3.6 \times 10^8 \times 3 \times 10^{-5}$
f $3.7 \times 10^{-10} \times 2 \times 10^4$
g $2 \times 10^{-2} \times 4 \times 10^{-4}$
h $7 \times 10^{-4} \times 2 \times 10^{-2}$
i $6.2 \times 10^{-6} \times 3 \times 10^{-10}$
j $6.6 \times 10^{-8} \times 4 \times 10^{-3}$

3 Write the following in standard form:

a $\dfrac{8 \times 10^7}{2 \times 10^4}$
b $\dfrac{15 \times 10^9}{3 \times 10^5}$

c $\dfrac{7 \times 10^6}{2 \times 10^3}$
d $\dfrac{3 \times 10^{10}}{4 \times 10^7}$

e $\dfrac{4 \times 10^4}{2 \times 10^7}$
f $\dfrac{9 \times 10^{-3}}{3 \times 10^2}$

g $\dfrac{20 \times 10^{-6}}{5 \times 10^3}$
h $\dfrac{2.5 \times 10^{-3}}{5 \times 10^7}$

i $\dfrac{16 \times 10^3}{4 \times 10^{-3}}$
j $\dfrac{2.7 \times 10^{-4}}{0.3 \times 10^{-2}}$

k $(5.4 \times 10^{-4}) \div (4.5 \times 10^{-11})$
l $(7.5 \times 10^{-8}) \div (15 \times 10^{-12})$

4   Estimate the value of:

   a $2.87 \times 10^{-3} \times 5.13 \times 10^4$

   b $(1.997 \times 10^5) \div (4.25 \times 10^{-2})$

   c $4.775 \times 10^{-7} \div (9.055 \times 10^{-10})$

   d $2.503 \times 10^3 \times 384$

   e $497 \div (9.89 \times 10^6)$

   f $2200 \times 1.343 \times 10^{-5}$

Give your answers in standard form.

> You can estimate a value by rounding each number to 1 significant figure.

5   Find:

   a $3.5 \times 10^3 + 1.6 \times 10^2$ b $2 \times 10^3 + 3 \times 10^3$

   c $2 \times 10^{-3} + 3 \times 10^{-3}$ d $5 \times 10^5 - 4 \times 10^4$

   e $3.1 \times 10^5 - 2.1 \times 10^4$ f $1.3 \times 10^{-3} - 4 \times 10^{-4}$

> Give your answers in standard form.

6   $a = 3 \times 10^{-3}$ and $b = 4 \times 10^{-4}$.

Find the following, giving your answers in standard form:

   a $a + 2 \times b$ b $100 \times b - a$

   c $\dfrac{a}{b}$ d b^2

> Replace a by 3×10^{-3} and b by 4×10^{-4}.
> So $a + 2 \times b$ becomes $3 \times 10^{-3} + 2 \times 4 \times 10^{-4}$

7   $P = 4 \times 10^1$ and $T = 5 \times 10^2$.

Work out the following, giving your answers in standard form:

   a $P \times T$ b $60 \times P + T$

   c $P^3 \div T^2$ d $\dfrac{T - 50 \times P}{T}$

6.7 Using a calculator

You can enter numbers in standard form into a scientific calculator without having to write them in full first.

Example 12

Use a calculator to find:

a $56\,400 + 5.79 \times 10^6$ **b** $3.057 \times 2.485 \times 10^{-15}$

a $56\,400 + 5.79 \times 10^6 = 5\,846\,400$

> Enter 5 6 4 0 0 + 5 . 7 9 EXP 6 =
> EXP is an abbreviation of **exponent**, which is another word for power or index. You enter only the power of 10, not 10 itself or the 'x' sign.

b $3.057 \times 2.485 \times 10^{-15} = 7.60 \times 10^{-15}$

   correct to 3 s.f.

> To enter a negative power, use the key that changes the sign of a number.
> Enter 3 . 0 5 7 × 2 . 4 8 5 EXP +/- 1 5 =
> The display shows 7.596645^{-15}. This means 7.596645×10^{-15}.

Read the manual for your calculator if the instructions given here do not work.

Exam practice 6G

1   Work out, correct to 3 significant figures:
   a $6 \times 1.571 \times 10^4$ **b** $12.5 \times 5.027 \times 10^3$
   c $0.45 \times 1.39 \times 10^{-4}$ **d** $6.78 \div (2.05 \times 10^5)$
   e $0.05575 \div (4.035 \times 10^{-3})$ **f** $205\,000 \div (5.8 \times 10^{10})$

2   Work out:
   a $2.179 \times 10^9 \div 3975$ **b** $4993 + 2.562 \times 10^4$
   c $0.2989 - 4.25 \times 10^{-2}$ **d** $0.7643 - 5.43 \times 10^{-2}$

3   Light travels 1 km in 3.3×10^{-6} seconds.
   How long does light take to travel 511 kilometres?

4   The distance travelled by light in a vacuum in one year is
   9.4650×10^{15} metres.
   How far does light travel in 1 second?

5   The mass of a proton is 1.67×10^{-24} grams and the mass of an
   electron is 9.11×10^{-28} grams.
   Find the difference between the mass of an electron and the
   mass of a proton.

6   In 2005, the Costwise supermarket chain baked 85 million
   loaves of bread and used 63 800 tonnes of flour.
   Work out the average weight of flour used in one loaf. Give your
   answer in grams.

7   The trustees of a pension fund invest £1.15×10^7.
   They predict the value of the fund in 9 years' time by
   multiplying this sum of money by $(1.041)^9$.
   Find the predicted value of the fund in 9 years' time.

8   When Jupiter, Pluto and the Sun are in line, Jupiter is
   7.88×10^8 km from the sun and Pluto is 5.95×10^9 km from
   the sun.
   What is the distance between Jupiter and Pluto when the two
   planets and the Sun are in line and when
   a   the planets are on opposite sides of the Sun
   b   the planets are on the same side of the Sun?

9   The amount of nitrate in one bottle of mineral water is
   1.3×10^{-2} grams and the amount of nitrate in another bottle
   of mineral water is 5.4×10^{-3} grams.
   Both bottles are emptied into one jug.
   How much nitrate is there in the water in the jug?

10   A clock ticks once a second.
   Work out how many years it takes to tick 1 billion times.

> Estimate your answer before you use a calculator. Use your estimate to check how reasonable your calculator answer is.

> Remember that (2.05×10^5) is a single number so brackets are not needed when using your calculator:

> This distance is called a light-year.

> You can do this in stages. Use 1 year = 365 days. Find how far light travels in 1 day, then in 1 hour, and so on.

> The EXP button can only be used for powers of 10. To find 1.041^9, enter 1.041 followed by the y^x button, then the power 9.

> 1 billion = 10^9.

Mini coursework task

10^{100} is called a googol.

10^{googol} is called a googolplex.

How many zeros does a googolplex have when it is written out in full?

Estimate the number of pages of lined A4 paper you would need to write this number in full.

Summary of key points

- When a, x and y are any numbers and a is not zero,
  1. $a^x \times a^y = a^{x+y}$
  2. $a^x \div a^y = a^{x-y}$
  3. $a^{-x} = \left(\dfrac{1}{a}\right)^x = \dfrac{1}{a^x}$
  4. $(a^x)^y = a^{xy}$
- Any number raised to the power zero equals 1.
- $a^{\frac{1}{n}} = \sqrt[n]{a}$ means the nth root of a. $2^{\frac{1}{2}} = \sqrt{2}$ and $2^{\frac{1}{3}} = \sqrt[3]{2}$.
- Numbers that cannot be expressed as $\dfrac{a}{b}$ where a and b are integers are called irrational numbers. Irrational numbers written like $\sqrt{2}$ and $\sqrt{7}$ are called surds.
- A number written in standard form is a number between 1 and 10 multiplied by a power of 10.
- When you multiply and divide numbers in standard form you do not need to write them in full. When a calculation involves addition or subtraction you must write numbers in full unless you use a calculator.

Most students who get GRADE C or above can:
- use index laws to multiply and divide integer powers of the same number
- recognise numbers in standard form on a calculator display.

Most students who get GRADE A or above can also:
- work with negative and fractional indices
- rationalise the denominator of a surd.

Glossary

Index (plural indices)	the small superscript number that tells you how many of the base are multiplied together
Exponent	another word meaning index
Irrational number	a number that cannot be expressed exactly as a fraction
Power	another word meaning index
Rational number	a number that can be written exactly as a fraction
Reciprocal	the number which when multiplied by the original number gives 1
Standard form	a number between 1 and 10 multiplied by a power of 10
Surd	an irrational number written as a root, such as $\sqrt{2}$ or $\sqrt{13}$

7 Measures

This chapter will show you:
- ✓ the common units used for measuring time, length, weight, capacity and temperature
- ✓ the relationships between different units for measuring a quantity
- ✓ compound measures such as speed and density
- ✓ how to convert between different currencies
- ✓ the range in which a rounded measurement lies and how to work with rounded numbers

Before you start you need to know:
- ✓ how to multiply and divide by 10, 100, 1000,...
- ✓ how to work with decimals, fractions and negative numbers
- ✓ how to round to a number of significant figures
- ✓ what a number in standard form means
- ✓ how to find the area of a rectangle
- ✓ how to find the volume of a cuboid

7.1 Length

Metric units of length in everyday use are
    kilometre (km),
    metre (m),
    centimetre (cm),
    millimetre (mm).

> The letters in the brackets show the abbreviations for these units.

The relationships between these units are
    1 kilometre = 1000 metres,
    1 metre = 100 centimetres = 1000 millimetres,
    1 centimetre = 10 millimetres.

> There are two systems of units that are used for length and weight. These are metric units and **Imperial units**.
>
> Metric units are the main units of measurement used in the United Kingdom.

You can use these relationships to convert the measurement of a length from one unit to another.

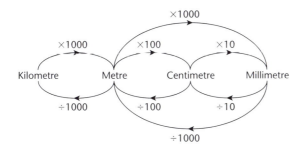

> To convert to a smaller unit, multiply because there are more of the smaller units in a given length.
>
> To convert to a larger unit, divide because there are fewer of the larger units in a given length.

Example 1

a Convert 10.5 cm into millimetres.
b Convert 10.5 cm into metres.

a   10.5 cm = 10.5 × 10 mm

   = 105 mm

> 1 cm = 10 mm, so
> 10.5 cm = 10.5 × 10 mm.

b   10.5 cm = 10.5 ÷ 100 m

   = 0.105 m

> 1 cm = $\frac{1}{100}$ m, so
> 10.5 cm = 10.5 ÷ 100 m.

The mile is the only Imperial unit of length that is still in everyday use in the UK.

Yards, feet and inches are other Imperial units of length that are used occasionally.

The relationships between these units are

   1 foot = 12 inches,
   1 yard = 3 feet,
   1 mile = 1760 yards.

You can convert between Imperial and metric units of length using

   5 miles ≃ 8 km,
   2 inches ≃ 5 cm,
   1 inch ≃ 2.54 cm.

> The symbol ≃ means is approximately equal to. It is used because these conversions are not exact.

Example 2

a   Convert 20 miles into kilometres.
b   Convert 44 cm into inches.

a $20 \times \frac{8}{5} = 32$

   20 miles is about 32 kilometres.

> 5 miles ≃ 8 km gives
> 1 mile ≃ $\frac{8}{5}$ km so to
> convert miles to km,
> multiply by $\frac{8}{5}$.

b $44 \times \frac{2}{5} = 17.6$

   44 cm is about 17.6 inches.

> 5 cm ≃ 2 in gives
> 1 cm ≃ $\frac{2}{5}$ in, so to
> convert cm to inches,
> multiply by $\frac{2}{5}$.

Units of area and volume

The metric units of area in everyday use are
   square metre (m²),
   square centimetre (cm²),
   square millimetre (mm²),
   hectare (ha), where 1 ha = 10 000 m².

> 1 m² is the area of a square with
> sides 1 m long. So 1 m²
> = 100 × 100 cm² = 10 000 cm².

The only Imperial unit of area still used is the acre.
You can convert between hectares and acres using 1 ha ≃ 2.5 acres.

The units of volume in everyday use are
   cubic metre (m³),
   cubic centimetre (cm³),
   cubic millimetre (mm³).

> 1 m³ is the volume of a cube with
> edges 1 m long.
> So 1 m³ = 100 × 100 × 100 cm³
>   = 1 000 000 cm³.

Exam practice 7A

1 **a** Kalik's bed is 2 metres long.
How many centimetres is this?
  b A fridge is 600 mm wide.
How many centimetres is this?

2 Hasim is 172 cm tall.
What is Hasim's height in metres?

3 Convert
  a 2.5 m to centimetres   **b** 693 mm to centimetres
  c 1.2 km to metres   **d** 4550 m to kilometres
  e 1536 mm to metres   **f** 0.25 km to metres.

4 Arrange the following lengths in order of size with the shortest
first.   25 m   156 cm   2889 mm   3.8 m   0.57 m

> You need all lengths in the same units.

5 Convert
  a 10 miles to km   **b** 40 miles to km
  c 80 km to miles   **d** 12 inches to cm
  e 40 cm to inches   **f** 2.4 acres to hectares.

6 Arrange these lengths in order of size with the longest first.
   24 inches, 1500 mm, 100 cm, 1 foot

> Start by writing all the lengths in the same unit.
> Remember that 1 foot = 12 inches.

7 When Ann goes to school she walks 450 m to the bus stop.
She then has a bus journey of 1.65 km followed by a walk of 130 m.
Work out the total distance that Ann travels to school.

> All quantities must be in the same units before you can add them.

8 The diameter of a pipe is $1\frac{1}{2}$ inches.
Find the diameter of the pipe in millimetres.
Use 1 inch = 25.4 mm.

9 A road sign in France gave the distance to Paris as 84 km.
1 km is equal to 0.621 miles.
Jordan said 'That means the distance is more than 50 miles.'
Is Jordan correct? Give a reason for your answer.

10 An old floor board is 6 inches wide.
The widths of new floor boards are given in millimetres.
Decide which of these widths can be used to replace the old board: 140 mm, 150 mm, 160 mm.
Use 1 inch = 25.4 mm.

11 Find 30 cm as a fraction of 3 feet.
Use 1 inch = 2.54 cm.

> To find one quantity as a fraction of another, write them both in the same unit, then place the first quantity over the second and simplify the fraction.

12 A plank is 2 cm thick.
When it is planed, 2.5 mm is taken off the thickness.
What fraction of the thickness is removed?

13 Graham said that 800 yards is more than $\frac{1}{2}$ mile.
Is Graham right? Explain your answer.

14 Emily knows her bedroom floor is a rectangle 10 feet wide and
12 feet long. She sees a rectangular carpet measuring 3.5 m by 4 m.
Will the carpet fit her bedroom floor?
Give a reason for your answer.

15 Freya has a rectangular carpet 3 feet wide and 4 feet 6 inches
long.
How much will it cost to have this carpet cleaned?

16 Tom knows that his living room ceiling is 10 feet 6 inches high.
The floor is a rectangle which Tom measures as 4.6 metres
long by 4.2 metres wide. Find the volume of the room in cubic
metres.

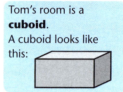

Tom's room is a
cuboid.
A cuboid looks like
this:

17 A rectangular field measures 400 m by 150 m.
What is the area of the field in hectares?

7.2 Mass

The main metric units for measuring mass are
tonne (t),
kilogram (kg),
gram (g).

The relationships between them are
1 tonne = 1000 kilograms,
1 kilogram = 1000 grams.

Mass is the scientific name for the amount
of matter in an object. In everyday language
we talk about the weight of something
rather than its mass. In science, weight is a
force caused by gravity and is measured in
Newtons.

You can use these relationships to convert a mass
given in one unit to another unit.

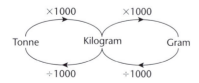

Did you know

that the exact weight of one kilogram is
measured against a kilogram weight made
in England out of platinum-iridium in
1889 and held in a sealed vault in Paris?
Over the years this weight has got lighter
because of microscopic surface abrasion.
The difference is about the same as a
single grain of sand.

All masses in the UK are now given in metric units.
Imperial units that are used occasionally are the ton,
the pound (lb) and the ounce (oz), where 1 lb = 16 oz.

You can convert, approximately, between kilograms
and pounds using
1 kg ≈ 2.2 lb.

Exam practice 7B

1 a A bag of potatoes weighs 2.5 kg. How many grams is this?
   b A crate is marked 4500 kg. How many tonnes is this?

2 Convert
   a 500 g to kilograms
   b 1.3 t to kilograms
   c 250 kg to tonnes
   d 1.35 kg to grams
   e 45 500 kg to tonnes
   f 12 000 g to tonnes.

3 Arrange the following weights in order of size with the lightest first.
       0.06 tonnes, 655 kg, 62 000 g

4 Convert
   a 5 kg to pounds   b 500 g to pounds   c 44 lb to kilograms.

5 Arrange the following weights in order of size, heaviest first.
       2.5 kg, 11 lb, 1500 g, 64 oz

> Convert the weights into the same units. Pounds is a convenient unit as it is easier to change kilograms to pounds than the other way round. Remember that 16 oz = 1 lb.

6 A bag of flour weighs 2.5 kg.
   David uses 500 g of this flour.
   What fraction of the flour in the bag does David use?

7 The weights of three parcels are 15.8 kg, 900 g and 48.5 kg.
   Work out the total weight of the parcels.

8 A bar of cooking chocolate weighs 100 g.
   1 ounce is equal to 28.4 grams.
   Is this bar enough to give 4 ounces of chocolate?
   Give a reason for your answer.

9 A complete pallet of bricks weighs 2.5 tonnes.
   One brick weighs 2.5 kilograms.
   Freda used 100 of these bricks to build a wall.
   Work out the fraction of the bricks on the pallet that Freda used.

7.3 Capacity

Capacity is used to measure the volume inside a container. It is also used as a measure of the volume of liquid.

Metric units of capacity in everyday use are
    litre (l),
    centilitre (cl),
    millilitre (ml).

> You will see 25 cl on some cans of soft drinks.

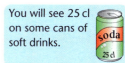

The relationships between these are
   1 litre = 100 centilitres = 1000 millilitres,
   1 centilitre = 10 millilitres.

A cubic centimetre is also a measure of volume:
   1 litre = 1000 cm³

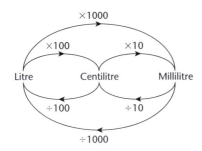

Gallons and pints are Imperial measures of capacity that are still used.
The relationship between them is 1 gallon = 8 pints.
You can use 1 gallon ≃ 4.5 litres to convert between gallons and litres.

 Exam practice 7C

1 a A container holds 10 litres of water.
      How many centilitres is this?
   b A can contains 30 cl of cola.
      What fraction of a litre is this?

2 Convert
   a 2 litres into millilitres   b 25 cl into millilitres
   c 500 ml into litres.

3 Arrange these capacities in order of size, largest first.
      0.46 litres, 50 cl, 400 ml, 0.05 litres, 40 ml

4 A coffee jug holds 2.5 litres when full.
   A cup holds 300 ml.
   How many cups can be filled from a full jug?

5 Arrange these capacities in order of size, smallest first.
      1 litre, 10 pints, 1 gallon.

 A01

6 The capacity of a watering can is marked in half gallons from
   1 to 5 gallons.
   A liquid fertiliser needs to be mixed with 10 litres of water.
   Which mark should the watering can be filled to?
   Explain whether your answer is exact or approximate.

7 A carton holds 0.8 litres of concentrated fabric conditioner.
   One wash needs 50 ml of this concentrate.
   How many washes will one carton give?

8 An old petrol tank holds 5 gallons.
   Use 1 gallon = 4.5 litres to find how many litres this tank will
   hold.

9 The capacity of an oil tank is 58 gallons.
   Use 1 gallon = 4.546 litres to estimate the capacity of the tank in
   litres.

 10 Kirsty buys an old oil tank. The tank is a cuboid with internal
   measurements 1.5 m by 1.5 m by 1 m.
   Kirsty is told that the tank holds 500 gallons.
   Is this correct? Give a reason for your answer.

7.4 Temperature

In Europe, temperature is usually measured in degrees Celsius.

> The freezing point of water is zero degrees Celsius, written as 0°C.
> The boiling point of water is 100 degrees Celsius, written as 100°C.

In the USA, temperature is usually measured in degrees Fahrenheit.

> The freezing point of water is 32 degrees Fahrenheit, written as 32°F.
> The boiling point of water is 212°F.

You can convert between these two temperature scales using these flow charts.

To convert from Fahrenheit to Celsius: °F → -32 → $\times 5$ → $\div 9$ → °C

To convert from Celsius to Fahrenheit: °C → $\times 9$ → $\div 5$ → $+32$ → °F

Exam practice 7D

1 Use the instructions above to convert
   a 20°C into degrees Fahrenheit
   b − 10°C into degrees Fahrenheit.

2 Use the instructions above to convert
   a 80°F into degrees Celsius   b 10°F into degrees Celsius.

3 In August 2003, the temperature in London reached a record
   high of 101°F. How many degrees Celsius is 101°F?

4 The instructions for converting a temperature of C degrees
   Celsius to F degrees Fahrenheit can be written as $F = \dfrac{9 \times C}{5} + 32$.

   Use these instructions to convert these temperatures into degrees
   Fahrenheit.   a 45°C   b 70°C   c 58°C

   > For part a you need to write 45 instead of C in the instructions.

5 The instructions for converting a temperature of F degrees
   Fahrenheit to C degrees Celsius can be written as $C = \dfrac{5(F - 32)}{9}$.

   Use these instructions to convert these temperatures into degrees
   Celsius.   a 250°F   b 100°F   c 82°F

7.5 Speed

When something moves it covers distance.
Speed measures the distance covered per unit of time.

Speed is a **compound measure** because it combines distance and time.

$$\textbf{average speed} = \frac{\textbf{total distance covered}}{\textbf{total time taken}}$$

The most common metric units of speed are kilometres per hour (km/h) and metres per second (m/s).

The only Imperial unit of speed in everyday use is miles per hour (mph).

> A car travels 80 miles in two hours. The car travels 40 miles each hour, so its speed is 40 mph (mph is short for miles per hour) .

> When you travel, your speed is likely to vary from time to time. You can give a speed for a whole journey by working out the average speed.

Example 3

Pedro walks 5 km in $1\frac{1}{2}$ hours.
a Find his average speed.
b Pedro stops for 10 minutes then walks a further 3 km in 50 minutes. Find Pedro's average speed for the whole of his journey.

a $5 \div 1\frac{1}{2} = 3.333\ldots$
Pedro's average speed is 3.3 km/h correct to one d.p.

b Total distance = 5 km + 3 km = 8 km ●——————— To find his average speed you need the distance and the total time.
Total time = $1\frac{1}{2}$ hours + 10 min + 50 min = $2\frac{1}{2}$ h ●——— To find the speed in kilometres per hour, you need the time to be in hours.
$8 \div 2\frac{1}{2} = 3.2$
Average speed = 3.2 km/h.

You can convert a speed given in one unit to another unit.

Example 4

Convert 10 km/h into   **a** mph   **b** m/s.

a $10 \times \frac{5}{8} = 6.25$ miles.
So 10 km/h $\approx$ 6.3 mph to 1 d.p.

> To convert kilometres to miles multiply by $\frac{5}{8}$.

b 10 km = 10 000 m ●———————
1 hour = 3600 s ●———————
So 10 km/h = 10 000 $\div$ 3600 m/s
= 2.8 m/s correct to 2 s.f.

> To convert 10 km/h to m/s, you need to convert kilometres to metres and divide by 60 $\times$ 60 to convert hours to seconds.

You can find the distance travelled when you know the speed and the time using

$$\textbf{distance} = \textbf{speed} \times \textbf{time}.$$

You can find the time when you know the distance and the speed using

$$\textbf{time} = \frac{\textbf{distance}}{\textbf{speed}}.$$

> This diagram will help you remember the relationships between distance, speed and time.
>
> Cover up the quantity you want to find.

Exam practice 7E

1 Find the average speed for each journey.
   a Robert cycled 30 km in 2 hours.
   b A train travelled 450 miles in 4 hours.
   c Keith took 30 minutes to walk 2 kilometres.
   d Greg drove 75 miles in $1\frac{1}{2}$ hours.
   e Tarik cycled 4.5 km in 10 minutes.
   f A bus took 30 minutes to travel 3 miles.
   g Val took 20 minutes to walk $1\frac{1}{4}$ miles.
   h Roger drove 50 miles in 75 minutes.

> You need to decide how accurate your answers should be and which units to use.

2 Fred shot an arrow at a target 90 metres away.
   The arrow was in flight for 2 seconds.
   Work out the average speed of the arrow in
   a metres per second   b kilometres per hour.

3 Nikki took 2 hours to drive 80 kilometres.
   Work out her average speed in metres per second.

4 Ali completed a half-marathon of 13 miles.
   He ran for 2 hours and walked for 30 minutes.
   Find Ali's average speed in miles per hour.

> To find a speed in metres per second, you need the distance in metres and the time in seconds.

5 Henry completed a marathon of 26 miles.
   His average speed was 6 mph.
   How long did it take Henry to complete the marathon?

6 The average speed of a car in the rush hour is 4 mph.
   How long does the car take to travel 6 miles at this speed?

7 The average speed of a rocket is 80 m/s.
   How long does it take the rocket to travel 2 kilometres?

8 Ann travels between London Waterloo and Brussels Midi.

LONDON	07:39	07:43	08:12	08:39	09:09	10:39	10:42	11:39	12:09	12:39	14:09
Ashford	08:29	—	—	09:30	09:59	—	—	—	12:59	13:30	14:59
Calais	—	—	—	10:56	—	—	—	—	14:31	—	—
Lille	—	—	—	11:29	—	—	13:24	14:21	—	15:29	—
BRUSSELS	—	11:03	—	12:10	—	—	14:05	—	—	16:10	—
PARIS	11:23	—	11:47	—	12:53	14:17	—	15:23	15:59	—	17:53

She catches the 1042 train from London Waterloo.
The distance between London and Brussels is 370 km.
   a Work out the average speed of the train assuming that it arrives on time.
   b The train arrives 30 minutes late. What was its average speed?

9 The distance of the Moon from the Earth is about 250 thousand miles.
Light travels at 1.86×10^5 miles a second.
How many seconds does it take for light to travel from the Moon to the Earth?

10 Light travels at 2.99×10^8 m/s.
Mars is 2.2794×10^8 km from the Sun.
Work out how many seconds it takes for light from the Sun to reach Mars.

11 The speed limit on motorways is 70 mph.
Use 1 mile = 1.61 km to convert this speed limit into km/h.

7.6 Density

Density measures the mass of one unit of volume of a material. The unit of volume usually used for density is the cubic centimetre (cm^3).

Density is a compound measure because it involves mass and volume.

You can work out density using $density = \dfrac{mass}{volume}$.

> Other units of volume that may be used are cubic millimetres (mm^3) and cubic metres (m^3).

Example 5

A block of wood has a mass of 400 grams and its volume is 500 cm^3.
Find the density of the wood.

500 cm^3 weighs 400 g,
$400 \div 500 = 0.8$ so 1 cm^3 weighs 0.8 grams.

> The density of the wood is the mass of 1 cubic centimetre.

The density of the wood is 0.8 g/cm^3.

> 0.8 g/cm^3 is the short way of writing 0.8 grams per cubic centimetre.

When you know the volume of an object and the density of the material from which it is made, you can work out its mass.

Example 6

The density of brass is 8.2 g/cm^3.
The volume of a block of brass is 500 cm^3. What does the block weigh?

$500 \times 8.2 = 4100$
So 500 cm^3 weighs 4100 g = 4.1 kg.

> The density tells you that 1 cm^3 weighs 8.2 grams. So 500 cm^3 weighs 500 times as much.

Exam practice 7F

1 A piece of oak has a volume of 4000 cubic centimetres.
   The density of oak is 0.8 g/cm³.
   Find the mass of this piece of oak.

2 The density of milk is 0.98 g/cm³.
   Work out the weight of 1 litre of milk.

1 litre = 1000 cm³

3 260 cubic centimetres of copper is used to make a pan.
   The density of copper is 8.9 g/cm³.
   Find the weight of the pan.

4 The volume of a gold bar is 32 cubic centimetres.
   The density of gold is 19.3 g/cm³.
   How much does the gold bar weigh?

5 A jug holds 500 cm³ of mercury.
   The density of mercury is 13.6 g/cm³.
   What is the mass of the mercury in the jug?

7.7 Exchange rates

Each country has its own units of money. The units of money are called **currencies**.

In the United Kingdom, the currency is pounds sterling and the symbol is £ where £1 = 100 pence.
In most parts of Europe, the currency is the Euro and the symbol is € where €1 = 100 cents.

You can convert one currency into another. To do this you need to know the **exchange rate**.
The exchange rate tells you what one unit of currency is equal to in another currency.

Several countries use the dollar as the name of their currency but they are not all worth the same amount.
The symbol for the dollar is $ where $1 = 100 cents.

The dollar symbol often has letters to distinguish between the different currencies. For example, US$ in the United States of America and NZ$ in New Zealand.

The exchange rates between most currencies change from day to day. This is because currencies can be bought and sold in the same way as, for example, houses or coffee.

Example 7

Use the exchange rate £1 = US$1.75 to convert
a   £2.50 into US dollars. (Give your answer to the nearest cent.)
b   US$25 into pounds sterling. (Give your answer to the nearest penny.)

a   £2.50 = US$ 2.50 × 1.75
          = US$ 4.375
          = US$ 4.38 to the nearest cent

Each £1 is worth 1.75 dollars so you convert £s to dollars by multiplying the number of £s by 1.75.

b   US$25 = £25 ÷ 1.75
          = £14.285…
          = £14.29 to the nearest penny

To convert dollars into £s you divide the number of dollars by 1.75.

Exam practice 7G

1 This table shows the exchange rates for some currencies.

   £1 = €1.69
   £1 = 2.68 Turkish lira (l)
   £1 = 1.80 US dollars

   a Freda changed £50 into Euros.
     How many Euros did she get?
   b Pete changed £200 into Turkish lira.
     Work out how many lira he got.
   c Jon changed £150 into US dollars. Find how many dollars he got.

   Give your answers to the appropriate degree of accuracy.

2 Jo paid a hotel bill for €500.
   The exchange rate was £1 = €1.58.
   Find the amount of the hotel bill in pounds.

3 Francis paid for a flight in Japan with his credit card.
   The exchange rate was 160 yen for £1.
   The amount on his statement was £500.
   What was the cost of the flight in Japanese yen?

4 Sally went to Australia.
   The exchange rate was £1 = 2.60 Australian dollars.
   a Sally bought a camera costing $500.
     Find the price of the camera in pounds.
   b Sally came home with 40 Australian dollars and changed them back into pounds.
     How many pounds did she get?

5 George went to France.
   He used £2 = €3 to get a rough idea of prices in pounds sterling.
   a George estimated that a CD cost £12.
     What was the price in Euros.
   b A pair of designer jeans cost 120 Euros.
     What did George estimate the price to be in pounds sterling?

6 Sonja changed £900 into Indian rupees.
   He got 55440 rupees.
   What was the exchange rate?

7 A bottle of water cost 48p in London.
   The same bottle of water cost €0.70 in Madrid when the exchange rate was €1.25 to the pound.
   In which city was the bottle of water cheaper?

8 Dennis went to Paris
   a Dennis changed £100 into Euros.
     He got €152.
     What was the exchange rate?
   b When Dennis got back to London, he changed €30 into pounds.
     He got £18.29.
     What was the exchange rate for this transaction?

9 Penny is going to Florida.
She goes to her bank to change some money into US dollars.
She sees this notice.
  a Penny changes £75 into US dollars.
     How much does she get?

BANK BUYS	BANK SELLS
US$ 1.90	US$ 1.70

  b When she gets back, how much will she get if she changes
     US$40 into sterling?

When you change £ to $, the bank is selling you dollars.

10 Pablo went to Spain.
He paid €250 for a pair of designer sunglasses.
Pierre went to Florida.
He paid US$280 for a pair of the same designer sunglasses.
The same sunglasses were on sale in London for £160.
Use £1 = $1.85 and £1 = €1.49 to find where these glasses were
cheapest.

7.8 The range in which a rounded number lies

When you round a number to a given number of significant figures,
you round up when the next significant figure is 5 or more and you
round down when it is less than 5.

Starting with a number that has been rounded, you can work
backwards to find its smallest possible value and its largest possible
value.

Example 8

250 people, to the nearest 10 people, get on to a ferry.
Find a the smallest number that can be on the ferry,
      b the largest number that can be on the ferry.

  a 245

The smallest number that can be rounded up to 250 is 5 less than 250.

  b 254

The largest number than be rounded down to 250 is up to, but not
including 5 more than 250. You can only have a whole number of people.

Measurements such as length and time do not take whole number
values only, they can have any value in a range.

Example 9

A line is 56 mm long correct to the nearest millimetre.
a Find the range in which this length lies.
b Illustrate the range on a number line.

a The line is from 55.5 mm up to but not
     including 56.5 mm long.
     If *a* mm is the length of the line then
         $55.5 \leqslant a < 56.5$.

> The lowest number that can be rounded up to 56 is 55.5.
> The highest number that can be rounded down to 56 is
> any number up to, but not including 56.5.
> The symbol $\leqslant$ means 'is less than or equal to'
> and $<$ means 'is less than'.

b  mm
     55.0   55.5   56.0   56.5   57.0

> The solid circle shows that 55.5 is included in
> the range and the open circle shows that 56.5 is
> not included.

In calculations you can use 56.5 mm as the greatest possible value
because 56.4999… mm = 56.5 mm when rounded to any number of
decimal places.

Working with rounded numbers

When you add, subtract, multiply or divide rounded numbers, you
are also adding, subtracting, multiplying and dividing the ranges in
which their possible values lie.

Example 10

Square tiles have sides that are 56 mm long to the nearest millimetre.
Ten of these square tiles are laid in a row.

Find the difference between the greatest and least possible length of
this row.

The least possible length of the row is 10 × 55.5 mm = 555 mm

The greatest possible length of this row is 10 × 56.5 mm = 565 mm

The difference between the greatest and least

possible length of the row is 10 mm.

> A side of one tile is at
> least 55.5 mm and at
> most 56.5 mm.

> This shows that the length of the row is only correct
> to the nearest 10 mm, so it is not as accurate as the
> length of one tile.
> Multiplying any corrected number will give an answer
> that is less accurate than the corrected number.
> This is why it is important that you do NOT correct
> any numbers until you have got to the end of the
> calculation.

Multiplying any rounded number will give an answer that is less
accurate. This is why you should never round any numbers until you
have got to the end of a calculation.

When adding or multiplying two rounded numbers:	When subtracting or dividing rounded numbers:
• the greatest possible result is when both numbers have their greatest possible values, • the smallest possible result is when both numbers have their least possible values.	• the greatest possible result is when the first number has its greatest value and the second number has its least value, • the least possible result is when the first number has its least possible value and the second number has its greatest possible value.

Example 11

Josh swam 50 metres in 45 seconds.
The length is correct to the nearest metre and the time is correct to the nearest second.
Find the greatest and least possible values of Josh's speed in km/h.

The distance is between 49.5 m and 50.5 m,

or 0.0495 km and 0.0505 km.

> For a speed in km/h, the distance must be in kilometres and the time in hours.

The time is between 44.5 sec and 45.5 sec

or $\dfrac{44.5}{3600}$ h and $\dfrac{45.5}{3600}$ h

The greatest possible speed = $0.0505 \div \dfrac{44.5}{3600}$ km/h = 4.09 km/h to 3 s.f.

The least possible speed = $0.0495 \div \dfrac{45.5}{3600}$ km/h = 3.92 km/h to 3 s.f.

Example 12

The numbers in this calculation are rounded to 3 significant figures.
$$\dfrac{45.6 - 23.1}{16.8 \times 1.66}$$
Find its least possible value.

Least possible value = $\dfrac{45.55 - 23.15}{16.85 \times 1.665}$ = 0.79842453…

> The numerator has to be as small as possible, and the denominator needs to be as large as possible.

Exam practice 7H

1 The weight of a bag of sand is 5.6 kg correct to 1 decimal place.
Find the range of values in which the weight lies.

2 A shop made a profit of £2500 one month.
This figure is correct to the nearest £100.
Find the smallest possible profit.

3 A metal pin in a hinge has to have a diameter of 1.25 mm to work properly. This diameter is correct to 2 decimal places.
Find the range in which the diameter must lie.

4 Dale measured the space between two kitchen units to the nearest centimetre. He wrote down 1.65 m.
   a   Write down the range within which the width of this space lies.
   b   Dale looked at a cupboard that he wanted to fit into the space.
The cupboard is 1651 mm wide.
Dale decided that the cupboard would not fit.
Explain why Dale could be wrong.

> Read the questions carefully. Make sure that you understand whether you are dealing with a quantity that can have any value within a range or a quantity that can only have whole number values.

A01

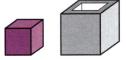

 5 The sides of a cube are 34 mm, correct to the nearest millimetre.
The inside of a box measures 34.2 mm by 34.2 mm
correct to 3 significant figures.
Explain why the cube might not fit in the box.

6 Knitting wool is sold by weight.
5 g of knitting wool has a length of 10 m correct to the nearest metre.
Work out the minimum length of wool in a 50 g ball.

7 The weight of a wall tile is 40 g to the nearest gram.
Work out the maximum weight of 250 of these tiles.

8 A box holds 200 nails, correct to the nearest 10 nails.
A shop has 50 boxes in stock. Find
a   the largest possible number of nails in stock
b   the smallest possible number of nails in stock.

9 A pair of digital scales gives weights correct to the nearest gram.
When one screw is weighed on these scales, the reading is 8 grams.
When 100 identical screws are weighed, the reading is 775 grams.
Give a more accurate weight for one screw.

10 A sheet of card is 58 cm long.
A strip of length 20 cm is cut from it.
Both measurements are correct to the nearest centimetre.
What is the greatest possible value of the length remaining?

> The difference between two numbers is greatest when the larger number is greatest and the smaller number is least.

11 John and Debbie both said that they were 15 years old.
What is the greatest possible difference in their ages?

12
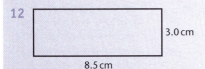
3.0 cm

8.5 cm

The measurements on this rectangular piece of card are correct to the nearest millimetre.
Find
a   the largest possible area of the card
b   the smallest possible area of the card.

 13 A one-penny coin has a diameter of 0.8 inches correct to 1 decimal place.
In a charity event, 80 000 of these coins are laid end to end in a line.
Josh says 'That line must be at least 1 mile long.'
Is he right?
Justify your answer. (1 mile = 63 360 inches)

14 A lorry can be loaded with 1.55 tonnes. This weight is correct to 3 significant figures.
Pallets, each weighing 120 kg to the nearest kilogram, are loaded on to the lorry.
How many pallets can be loaded?

15 Dale ran 3 kilometres in 20 minutes and then walked 2 kilometres in 20 minutes.
The distances are correct to the nearest 10 metres and the times are correct to the nearest minute.
Find the greatest possible value of Dale's average speed for the journey.

For speed in km/h, the distance must be in kilometres and the time in hours.

16 Winston measured his height as 5 feet 10 inches to the nearest inch.
1 inch = 2.54 cm correct to 3 significant figure.
Find, in metres, the range in which Winston's height lies.

17 The measurements on this box are correct to the nearest millimetre.

Find the greatest possible volume of the box.

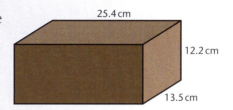

25.4 cm

12.2 cm

13.5 cm

18 One cubic metre of packing material is made from foam with a density of $0.12 \, \text{g/cm}^3$ correct to 2 decimal places.
The volume is correct to the nearest hundredth of a cubic metre.
Find the maximum possible weight of this foam.

19 The numbers in each calculation are correct to 3 significant figures. Find the greatest possible value of each calculation.

Write down all the figures in your calculator display.

a $\dfrac{2.77 \times 12.8}{41.5 - 37.8}$ b $\dfrac{250^2}{125 \times 21.9}$ c $\dfrac{2.08}{25.6(17.1 - 16.9)}$

20 The figures in this calculation are correct to 2 significant figures.

$$\frac{1.5 \times 10^3 - 4.8 \times 10^2}{37 + 46}$$

Find the difference between its greatest and least possible values.

Summary of key points

- The relationships between the main metric units of length are given in this diagram.

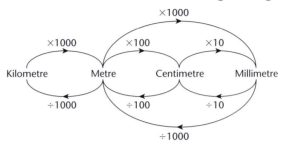

- The relationships between the main metric units of mass are given in this diagram.

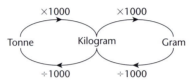

- The relationships between the main metric units of capacity are given in this diagram.

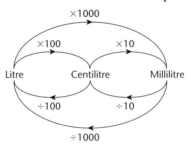

- 1 litre = 1000 cm^3
- You multiply when you convert to a smaller unit, e.g. metres to millimetres.
- You divide when you convert to a larger unit, e.g. grams to kilograms.
- You can convert between metric and Imperial units using
  5 miles $\simeq$ 8 kilometres, 10 cm $\simeq$ 4 inches, 1 kg $\simeq$ 2.2 lb, 1 gallon $\simeq$ 4.5 litres.
- Temperature is measured in degrees Celsius or in degrees Fahrenheit. You can convert between them using these flowcharts.

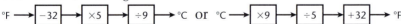

- Speed is measured in kilometres an hour (km/h), metres a second (m/s) or miles an hour (mph).
- You can use the diagram to find the relationships between distance, time and speed. Cover up the one you want to find.
- You can find the density of a material by dividing the volume of a quantity of it by its mass.
- You can change an amount in pounds to an amount in another currency by multiplying by the exchange rate.
- You can change an amount in another currency back to pounds by dividing by the exchange rate.
- The actual value of a rounded number lies within a range of values.
- When you calculate with rounded numbers, the accuracy of the result changes.

Most candidates who get GRADE C or above can:
- convert between the common units of measure
- find the range in which a corrected number lies.

Most candidates who get GRADE A or above can also:
- find the maximum or minimum value of the difference or sum of rounded numbers.

Glossary

Average speed	total distance ÷ total time
Capacity	the amount that a container will hold
Cuboid	a solid with six rectangular faces:
Currency	unit of money
Density	the mass of one unit of volume of a material
Compound measure	a unit that involves two or more simple units
Exchange rate	how much of one currency you will get for one unit of another
Imperial units	a set of units used to measure length, mass and capacity; only the mile and the pint are still officially in use in the United Kingdom
Mass	the amount of matter in an object; called weight in everyday language
Metric units	a set of units used to measure length, mass and capacity
Speed	the distance covered in one unit of time

8 Percentages

8.1 Converting percentages, fractions and decimals

The word **percent** means 'out of 100'.
Percentages are fractions with **denominators** of 100.
To write a percentage as a fraction, put the percentage over 100 and remove the percentage sign.

> 20 percent means 20 out of 100, or $\frac{20}{100}$.
> The symbol % is used for the word 'percent'.
> 5% means $\frac{5}{100}$, and 76% means $\frac{76}{100}$.

Example 1

Write these percentages as fractions in their lowest terms.

a 15%   b 44%

a $15\% = \frac{15}{100} = \frac{3}{20}$

b $44\% = \frac{44}{100} = \frac{11}{25}$

> Write the percentage as a fraction with denominator 100 then simplify.

To express a percentage as a decimal, write it as a fraction then divide the numerator by the denominator.

So $5\% = \frac{5}{100} = 0.05$

and $12.5\% = \frac{12.5}{100} = 0.125$

> To divide by 100, move the digits 2 places to the right.

The number in the decimal is 100 times smaller than the number in the percentage.

To write a percentage as a decimal, divide by 100 and remove the percentage sign.

To express a decimal as a percentage you need to write it as a fraction with a denominator of 100.

You can do this easily with a decimal because the decimal places give numbers of tenths, hundredths, and so on.

$$0.25 = \frac{25}{100} = 25\%$$

Divide top and bottom by 10 to give a denominator of 100.

$$1.125 = 1\frac{125}{1000} = \frac{1125}{1000} = \frac{112.5}{100} = 112.5\%$$

Change to an improper fraction.

There is a shortcut for this.
Looking at 0.25 = 25% and 1.125 = 112.5%, you can see that the number in the percentage is 100 times the number in the decimal.

To write a decimal as a percentage, multiply the decimal by 100 and add a percentage sign.

A fraction is another way of writing a decimal.

To write a fraction as a percentage, multiply the fraction by 100 and add a percentage sign.

Example 2

Write these fractions as percentages.　**a** $\frac{3}{8}$　**b** $\frac{1}{3}$

a　$\frac{3}{8} = \frac{3}{8} \times 100\% = \frac{300}{8}\% = 37.5\%$

b　$\frac{1}{3} = \frac{1}{3} \times 100\% = \frac{100}{3}\% = 33.3\%$ (to 3 s.f.)

Exam practice 8A

1　Write the following percentages as decimals:
　　a 14%　　　　　**b** 130%　　　　　**c** 17.5%
　　d 45.75%　　　**e** 0.6%

2　Write these percentages as fractions in their lowest terms:
　　a 25%　　　　　**b** $12\frac{1}{2}\%$　　　　**c** 110%

Write $12\frac{1}{2}$ as an improper fraction.

3　Convert these decimals into percentages:
　　a 0.54　　　**b** 0.8　　　**c** 1.05　　　**d** 0.05

4　Write the following fractions as percentages:
　　a $\frac{5}{8}$　　**b** $\frac{3}{4}$　　**c** $1\frac{1}{2}$　　**d** $\frac{1}{6}$　　**e** $\frac{2}{3}$　　**f** $1\frac{1}{3}$

5　Copy this table and fill in the blank spaces.

Fraction	Percentage	Decimal
$\frac{7}{20}$		
	65.5%	
		2.785
	125%	

8.2 Using a calculator

Many calculations do not work out exactly when you use decimals.

> You need to be aware of this when you use a calculator. Use fractions when you need an exact answer.

Example 3

Write $\frac{1}{3}$ as a percentage correct to 2 decimal places.

$\frac{1}{3} = \frac{1}{3} \times 100\% = 33.333...\% = 33.33\%$ correct to 2 d.p.

> Work to 3 d.p. and round your answer to 2 d.p.

Exam practice 8B

1   Write the following as percentages:

  a $\frac{1}{12}$ b $\frac{5}{9}$ c $3\frac{2}{15}$

  Give your answers correct to 1 decimal place.

> Use a calculator only when you cannot easily and quickly work without it.

2   Write the following as percentages:

  a $1\frac{2}{3}$ b $2\frac{1}{6}$ c $\frac{7}{12}$

  Give your answers exactly.

> You will need to use mixed numbers to give your answers exactly.

3   Joy spends $\frac{5}{12}$ of her income on rent.
  What percentage of her income is this?

4   Work out the percentage off the marked price.

> SPECIAL OFFER
> $\frac{1}{3}$ OFF
> marked price

5   Colin's wage is £260. £75 is taken off his wage for tax.
  a   Work out the tax as a fraction of his wage.
  b   Convert this fraction to a percentage.

6   The price of a laptop computer is £450 plus $17\frac{1}{2}\%$ VAT
  Express $17\frac{1}{2}\%$ as a decimal.

> **Did you know**
> that **Value Added Tax (VAT)** is a tax which is added to most things you buy?

A01   7   Stella said '33% off is the same as $\frac{1}{3}$ off.'
  Is Stella correct? Give a reason for your answer.

8.3 Finding a percentage of a quantity

You know how to find a fraction of a quantity.
You can find a percentage of a quantity by finding 1% and multiplying by the percentage needed.

Example 4

Find 3% of £12.

> 1% of £12 = £12 ÷ 100 = £0.12
> 3% = £0.12 × 3 = £0.36 or 36p.

> First find 1% of £12.
> 1% = $\frac{1}{100}$,
> so 1% of £12 = £12 ÷ 100.

There are some short cuts that help you to work out common percentages of a quantity.

50% = $\frac{1}{2}$, 25% = $\frac{1}{4}$, 75% = $\frac{3}{4}$, $33\frac{1}{3}$% = $\frac{1}{3}$, 10% = $\frac{1}{10}$

> Remember these facts.

Example 5

Find: **a** 10% of 80 g   **b** 25% of £48   **c** $33\frac{1}{3}$% of 18 cm

a 10% of 80 g = $\frac{1}{10}$ of 80 g = $\frac{1}{10}$ × 80 g = 8 g

b 25% of £48 = $\frac{1}{4}$ of £48 = $\frac{1}{4}$ × £48 = £12

c $33\frac{1}{3}$% of 18 cm = $\frac{1}{3}$ of 18 cm = $\frac{1}{3}$ × 18 cm = 6 cm

Exam practice 8C

1 Find:
   a 25% of £80   **b** 10% of 30p   **c** 20% of £6.50
   d 50% of £86   **e** 60% of £440   **f** 15% of £26

2 Find:
   a 5% of £360   **b** 200% of £250
   c 150% of £300   **d** $12\frac{1}{2}$% of 400 m
   e $7\frac{1}{2}$% of 3000 litres   **f** $2\frac{1}{2}$ % of £75 000

3 A builder gives an estimate of £2500 for a job.
   VAT of $17\frac{1}{2}$% of the estimate has to be added.
   Work out the VAT.

4 Roger buys a book on the Internet priced £7.80.
   There is a delivery charge of 5% of the price.
   Find the delivery charge.

5 Holly sells her house for £250 000.
   The Estate Agent charges $2\frac{1}{2}$% of the sale price.
   How much does the estate agent charge?

Class discussion

You can find 10% of a quantity by dividing by 10.
How can you use this to find each of these?

5%

15%

$2\frac{1}{2}$%

$7\frac{1}{2}$%

$17\frac{1}{2}$%

6   VAT of 5% is added to an electricity bill.
    What is the VAT on a bill of £84.50?

7   Shelly gets a salary of £22 000 a year.
    She pays no tax on the first £5000 of this.
    She pays 10% on the next £2000 and 20% on the remainder
    Work out the amount of tax that Shelly pays.

8   Find:

    a   83% of £240   b $17\frac{1}{2}$% of £14.25
    c $117\frac{1}{2}$% of £200   d   2.3% of £2400
    e   4.27% of £589   f   36.7% of 454 g
    g   16.7% of 21 cm   h   23% of 650 people
    i   103% of 65 miles   j   130% of 5 minutes

> You can use a calculator to find 83% of £240 by pressing
> 2 4 0 × 8 3 % = .

9   The floor area of a supermarket is 1500 square metres.
    8.5% of this floor area is used for selling clothes.
    Find the floor area used for selling clothes.

10 Jack buys a printer priced at £89.90 plus VAT.
    VAT is $17\frac{1}{2}$% of the price. Work out the VAT.

11 Summer bought a car for £4500.
    Five years later, she sold her car for 48% of what she had paid
    for it. Find the amount Summer sold her car for.

12 These are some of the results of the 2001 national census.
    The population of the UK was 58 789 194 people.

    a   21% of the population was over 60 years old.
        Work out the number of people who were over 60 years old.

    b   8.6% of the population lived in Scotland.
        How many people lived in Scotland?

13 There are 580 students in a school.
    57% of the students are girls.
    How many of the students are boys?

14 Helen bought 500 pens.
    She sold 75% of them for 12p each.
    She sold 80% of the remaining pens for 10p each.
    She gave the rest of the pens away.
    Work out the amount of money Helen got from these pens.

 15 Dennis said 'If two of us buy rail tickets
    we will save 60%.'
    Explain why he is wrong.

Gold Travel Card

30% off all standard fares

8.4 Finding one quantity as a percentage of another

You know how to find one quantity as a fraction of another.
You can find one quantity as a percentage of another by first finding
it as a fraction, then converting the fraction to a percentage.

Example 6

Find £13 as a percentage of £80.

£13 is $\frac{13}{80}$ of £80
$\frac{13}{80} = 0.1625 = 16.25\%$
so £13 is 16.25% of £80.

Exam practice 8D

1   Write
    a   £2.50 as a percentage of £80
    b   45 cm as a percentage of 1 metre
    c   2 ml as a percentage of 20 cl
    d   15p as a percentage of £1.50.

> To find one quantity
> as a fraction of
> another make sure
> both quantities have
> the same units.

2   Find   a   35 marks as a percentage of 60 marks
            b   74p as a percentage of £1.11
            c   £4.50 as a percentage of £4
            d   80 seconds as a percentage of 1 minute.

3   Twenty cars went through an MOT one day.
    Six of these cars failed. Work out the percentage that failed.

4   A pair of shoes is in a sale. They were originally priced £38.50.
    Find the £10 off as a percentage of the marked price of this pair
    of shoes.

> **SALE**
> £10 off all marked prices

5   There were 2300 applications for tickets for a concert.
    Only 580 tickets were available.
    Work out the percentage of applications that got tickets.

6   Valda put £750 into an income bond.
    She got £26.25 income from this bond.
    Find the income as a percentage of the money Valda put into the
    bond.

7   Jason ordered groceries on the Internet.
    The cost of the groceries was £64 and there was a £5 delivery
    charge.
    Find the delivery charge as a percentage of the cost of his
    groceries.

8   In a survey of 2000 people, 480 said they did not own a car.
    What percentage of the people surveyed said they did not own a
    car?

9   Kate put £460 into a savings account.
    After two years, there was £502 in the account.
    Find £502 as a percentage of £460.

8.5 Percentage increase and decrease

**A percentage used to describe
an increase or a decrease
is always a percentage of the
quantity before it is changed.**

Percentages are often used to describe increases and decreases.
For example, 'Average council tax increases are 8% this year.'
'Computer prices have decreased by 20% over the last 3 years.'

Example 7

A bus fare is 80p now, and will increase by 5% next month.
Find the new fare.

This means that the
increase is 5% of 80p.

1% of 80p = 80p ÷ 100 = 0.8p
so 5% of 80p = 5 × 0.8p = 4p
80 + 4 = 84 so the new fare is 84p.

You can work out the new fare directly without first finding the
increase.
The new fare is 5% more than the present fare, so the increased fare is
$100\% + 5\% = 105\%$ of the present fare.
Increased fare = 105% of 80p
$$= \tfrac{105}{100} \times 80p = 1.05 \times 80p = 84p.$$

This is called a **multiplier**.

The multiplier that
increases a quantity is
(100% + percentage
increase) expressed as
a decimal.
So the multiplier to
increase a quantity
by 15% is 115%
expressed as a
decimal, or 1.15.

When a quantity is decreased by a percentage, you can find the
decreased quantity in the same way.

Example 8

A new car cost £8500. In the first year it lost 20% of its value. Find its
value after one year.

Its value decreased by
20% of £8500.

1% of £8500 = £8500 ÷ 100 = £85
so 20% of £8500 = 20 × £85 = £1700
Value after one year = £8500 − £1700 = £6800.

You can work out the value after one year directly.
It is 20% less than the new cost.
So the value after one year is 100% − 20% = 80% of the new cost.
Decreased value = 80% of £8500

$$= \frac{80}{100} \times £8500 = 0.8 \times £8500 = £6800.$$

This is the multiplier.

> The multiplier that decreases a quantity is (100% – the percentage decrease) expressed as a decimal.
> So the multiplier to decrease a quantity by 25% is 100% − 25% = 75% = 0.75.

Using multipliers to increase or decrease a quantity is a direct way to find the changed quantity.

> Make sure you do not use multipliers to find just the increase or decrease.

Example 9

Greg bought a car priced at £12650.
He was given a discount of £1500.
Find the percentage discount.

$\dfrac{1500}{12650}$ = 0.11857… = 11.86% correct to 2 decimal places.

Greg was given a discount of 11.86%.

Exam practice 8E

1 a Write down the multiplier that increases a quantity by
      i 8%   ii 35%   iii $17\frac{1}{2}$%.
   b Write down the multiplier that decreases a quantity by
      i 12%   ii 15%   iii 4.25%.

2 Tim's weight increased by 12% between his fifteenth and sixteenth birthdays. He weighed 65 kg on his fifteenth birthday. What did he weigh on his sixteenth birthday?

3 a Grace's water rates are 6% more this year than they were last year. She paid £510 last year. How much are Grace's water rates this year?
   b A man's suit is usually priced at £125.
      This price is reduced by 20% in a sale. Find the sale price.

4 a Last year, 540 children went to the village school.
      There are 8% fewer children at the school this year.
      How many children are there this year?
   b There are 800 pupils in the school this year.
      Next year there will be 40 more pupils in the school.
      Work out the percentage increase in the number of pupils.

5 a Misty used to earn £280 a week.
      She now works fewer hours and earns £245 a week.
      Find the percentage reduction in her earnings.
   b A factory employs 220 workers.
      Next year the work force will be increased by 15%.
      How many workers will be employed next year?

> Read the questions carefully. Make sure that you know whether you are asked to find the changed amount or just the increase or decrease. Also make sure that you know if you are asked to find a quantity or a percentage.

6   a   A bathroom suite is labelled at £850.
        VAT is added at $17\frac{1}{2}$% of the marked price to give the selling
        price.
        Work out the amount Stan has to pay to buy this suite.
    b   A CD costs £7 plus value added tax at 20% of the cost price.
        How much has to be paid for the CD?

7   There were 36 reported cases of measles last year in the local
    health area.
    This year the number of reported cases has dropped by 15%.
    a   How many cases have been reported this year?
    b   How many fewer cases is this than last year?

8   Mrs Brown buys 150 theatre tickets priced at £18 each.
    She is given a discount of 12%.
    Work out what Mrs Brown pays for the tickets.

9   Khalid bought 120 bottles of water for £54.
    He sold them for 60p each. Find his percentage profit.

10 Rob bought 2000 packs of envelopes for £1200.
    He sold 750 packs for £1 each.
    He sold the rest of the packs for 50p each.
    a   Did Rob make a profit or a loss on these envelopes?
        Give a reason for your answer.
    b   Work out the percentage profit or loss.

> Profit is the difference between the buying price and the selling price. So the percentage profit is the profit as a percentage of the cost.

11 A bookshop has this offer.
    Raj bought 3 books. The prices were £5.99, £7.55, £6.99.
    Find his percentage saving.

> **3 FOR 2**
> BUY 3 BOOKS AND GET
> THE CHEAPEST ONE
> *FREE*

12 When Ben drives at 40 mph, he does 12 miles on each litre of
    petrol.
    When he drives at 50 mph, the number of miles he does on a
    litre of petrol decreases by 25%.
    Work out the number of litres per mile Ben uses when he drives
    at 50 mph.

13 When petrol was 80p per litre Sam used 700 litres in a year.
    The price rose by 12% so Sam reduced his yearly consumption
    by 12%.
    a   Find the new price of a litre of petrol.
    b   Work out Sam's new yearly petrol consumption.
    c   What is the change in Sam's petrol bill for the year as
        i a sum of money   ii a percentage?

14 A hospice has a fund raising team.
    15% of the £45 600 raised in 2003 went on costs.
    The hospice kept the rest.
    They raised 12% less money in 2004 but reduced the costs by 10%.
    Work out the amount of money the hospice kept from fund
    raising in 2004.

8.6 Finding the original quantity

You can find the original quantity when you know the percentage change and the final value.

Example 10

A chair cost £65.99 after an increase of 10%. Find the original price.

1.1 × (original price) = £65.99

So original price = £65.99 ÷ 1.1
= £59.99 to the nearest penny.

> The multiplier that increases the original price by 10% is 1.10, or 1.1

> Divide both sides by 1.1.

Example 11

The price of a shirt is £8.60 after a reduction of $12\frac{1}{2}$%. Find the original price.

0.875 × (original price) = £8.60

So original price = £8.60 ÷ 0.875
= £9.83 to the nearest penny.

> The multiplier that reduces a quantity by $12\frac{1}{2}$% is
> $(100 - 12.5)$%
> $= 87.5\% = 0.875$.

You can find the original quantity by dividing the final quantity by the multiplier that changed it.

Exam practice 8F

1 The price of a hair dryer is £13.80. This price includes VAT at $17\frac{1}{2}$%.
   Find the price before VAT was added.

2 A computer cost £763.75 including VAT at $17\frac{1}{2}$%.
   Find the price before VAT was added.

3 30% of Joe's pay is deducted for tax and pension contributions.
   He got £182 last week. Work out his pay before the deduction.

4 Water increases in volume by 4% when frozen.
   How much water is needed to make 900 cm³ of ice?

5 The stretched length of an elastic rope is 54 cm.
   This is 26% more than its natural length.
   What is the natural length of this rope?

6 A bottle of water costs 85p in a shop.
   This is 20% more than the shop paid for it.
   Find what the shop paid for the bottle of water.

7 Amin was paid £37 500 a year after an increase of $5\frac{1}{2}\%$.
   Work out what Amin was paid before the increase.

8 A DVD recorder is priced £167.50.
   This price is 3.5% more than it was this time last year.
   What was the price a year ago?

9 A set of cutlery is sold at a discount of 15% in a sale.
   The sale price is £59.49.
   a Find the pre-sale price.
   b Work out the discount.

10 Jane works overtime and increases her pay to £250 a week.
    This is a 15% increase on her normal pay.
    a Find her normal pay.
    b How much was Jane paid for overtime work?

11 A printer costs £102 including VAT at $17\frac{1}{2}\%$.
    Work out the VAT.

12 Tom buys a CD in France.
    It cost €15 including VAT of 20%. Work out the VAT.

13 Sally is given a pay rise of 2.5%.
    After the pay rise, she is paid £22 400 a year.
    Find the amount of the increase.

14 The price of a house has risen by 15% in one year.
    It is now valued at £150 000.
    Find the increase in its value.

8.7 Compound percentage change

Quantities can have several percentage changes, one after the other.
This is called compound percentage change.

Example 12

A camera is priced £290 + VAT at 17½%.
There is a discount of 5% before VAT for a cash payment.
Find the total cash price.

Cash price before VAT is added = 0.95 × £290

Cash price including VAT = 1.175 × (0.95 × £290) including VAT

= £323.71 to nearest penny

> First you have to reduce £290 by 5%.
> The multiplier is 0.95.

> You have to increase the result by $17\frac{1}{2}\%$. The multiplier is 1.175.

> You can use your calculator to work out the cash price in one step.
> Press 1 . 1 7 5 × 0 . 9 5 × 2 9 0 = .

Interest

When you put money into a savings account, you will be paid a sum of money called **interest**. This sum is a percentage of the amount in the account and it is usually paid yearly.

When you borrow money, you will have to pay a sum of money over and above the amount you borrowed. This is also called interest.

Interest that is paid on the same amount each year is called **simple interest**.

Example 13

Sally has £3500 in a savings account that pays simple interest of 4.5% p.a. How much interest will she earn in **a** 1 year   **b** 5 years?

> p.a. is short for 'per annnum' and means each year.

a Simple interest for 1 year on £3500 at 4.5% = 4.5% of £3500

$\qquad\qquad\qquad\qquad\qquad\qquad$ = £3500 × 0.045

$\qquad\qquad\qquad\qquad\qquad\qquad$ = £157.50

> 4.5% = 0.045

b Simple interest for 5 years = 5 × £157.50

$\qquad\qquad\qquad\qquad\qquad\quad$ = £787.50

If you do not withdraw money (or pay off a loan) **compound interest** is paid.
With compound interest, the interest is added to the amount at the end of the year. So the following year there is interest on an increased amount.

Example 14

Aynsley put £4500 in an account that paid 5.5% p.a. compound interest.
a How much is in the account after   **i** 1 year   **ii** 3 years?
b What was the compound interest after 3 years?

a **i** After one year the amount in the account = 1.055 × £4500

$\qquad\qquad\qquad\qquad\qquad\qquad\qquad\qquad$ = £4747.50

> The multiplier that increases a quantity by 5.5% is 1.055.

$\quad$ **ii** After two years the amount = 1.055 × (1.055 × £4500)

$\quad$ **iii** After three years the amount = 1.055 × [1.055 × (1.055 × £4500)]

$\qquad\qquad\qquad\qquad\qquad\qquad\qquad$ = $(1.055)^3$ × £4500

$\qquad\qquad\qquad\qquad\qquad\qquad\qquad$ = £5284.09 to the nearest penny

b The compound interest = amount after 3 years − original amount

$\qquad\qquad\qquad\qquad\qquad\qquad\quad$ = £5284.09 − £4500

$\qquad\qquad\qquad\qquad\qquad\qquad\quad$ = £784.09

This is the **compound interest**.

> The brackets show you where each step in the reasoning comes from. They are not needed for the calculation, so you can work this out in one step on your calculator.

Example 15

Peter invests £5000 in a savings account paying 4% p.a. compound interest. How long does he need to leave it there so that it grows to more than £5500?

> After 1 year, there is 1.04 × £5000 = £5200 in the account.
>
> After 2 years, there is 1.04 × £5200 = £5408 in the account.
>
> After 3 years there is 1.04 × £5408 = £5624.32 in the account.
>
> This is more than £5500, so the money has to be left for three years.

> Work out the changed amount each year until it is greater than £5500.
> The multiplier that increases a quantity by 4% is 1.04.

Exam practice 8G

1 Jim's weekly wage last year was £250. This was increased by 2% in January, and in June the new wage was increased by 1.5%. What is Jim's weekly wage after the second increase?

> The numbers given in the question are estimates so your answers can only be estimates. This means that a reasonable degree of accuracy is to give answers to the nearest thousand.

2 The population of oyster-catchers on Eden Island decreases by 15% each year.
   The present population is estimated to be 12 000 pairs.
   What is the estimated population in
   a a year's time
   b 2 years' time?

3 A new car costs £10 000.
   It depreciates by 20% in the first year and then by 15% of its remaining value in the second year.
   a Find its value
      i after 1 year   ii after 2 years.
   b Work out the loss in value after two years.

4 Mr Connah weighed 115 kg when he started a diet.
   He lost 10% of his weight in the first month and 8% of his reduced weight in the second month.
   What did he weigh after 2 months of dieting?

5 In any year the value of a motorbike depreciates by 10% of its value at the beginning of that year.
   Rene paid £3400 for a new motorbike two years ago.
   Work out its value now.

A01 6 Greg ordered £100 worth of goods online.
   He expected to pay £80 but was charged £81.
   a Explain why you think that Greg expected to pay £80.
   b Give reasons why the company can justify the charge of £81.

Order this month and we will give you 10% discount.
Order online and we will give you a further 10% discount

7 a Freda puts £350 into a bond that pays interest at 5.4% p.a.
      Find the compound interest on this bond after 3 years.
   b Sean puts £350 into an account that pays interest at 5.4% p.a. and takes the interest out each year.
      How much interest does he get in 3 years?

8 Find the compound interest on
   a £6000 invested for 3 years at 3.5% p.a.
   b £7500 invested for 4 years at 5% p.a.
   c £12 000 invested for 4 years at 4.25%.

9 Don buys a house for £160 000.
   The value of the house appreciates at 8% a year.
   Work out what the house will be worth in 2 years' time.

'appreciates' means 'goes up'.

10 Three years ago Helen bought a rare postage stamp for £50.
    Each year its value increased by 15%.
    What is the stamp worth now?

11 It costs £4.50 for a car to cross a toll bridge.
    This cost will increase by 5% a year rounded down to the
    nearest 10 pence.
    Work out the cost for a car to cross the bridge
    a after the second increase   b after the third increase.

'Rounded down to the nearest 10' means that 28, 25, 22 and 20 are all rounded to 20.

12 A new lorry costs £60 000.
    It will lose 15% of its value in the first year.
    Every year after the first year it will lose 10% of its value at the
    start of that year.
    Work out the value of the lorry when it is three years old.

13 A new motorbike cost £9000.
    Each year it loses 20% of its value at the beginning of that year.
    a Find its value after 3 years.
    b Work out the percentage decrease in its value over the 3 years.

14 When a ball is dropped, the height of each bounce is 10% less
    than the height of the previous one.
    The first bounce was 150 cm high.
    How high did the ball go after its fourth bounce?

15 David put £30 000 into a savings account.
    The interest for the first year was 5.5%, the interest for the second
    year was 4.8% and the interest for the third year was 4.5%.
    David did not draw any money out of the account and he did
    not put any in.
    Find the amount in the account after 3 years.

16 The amount that a person can earn each year without having to
    pay income tax is £5000.
    This amount, rounded up to the nearest £10, will increase at the
    rate of inflation.
    The expected rates of inflation are given in the table.

Number of years from now	1	2	3	4	5
Expected rate of inflation	3%	2.5%	4.5%	4.8%	5.3%

Use these values to find the tax-free amount a person can earn
in 5 years' time.

17 The population of Tiverly has grown by 4% a year for the last 3 years.
It is expected to increase at the same rate over the next 3 years.
The present population of Tiverly is 15 000.
  a Work out what the population was 2 years ago.
  b Estimate what the population will be in 3 years' time.
  c How many years will it take for the population to grow to more than 18 000?

18 A computer system is valued at £50 000 now.
By the end of the year it will lose 30% of its value.
After that it will lose 20% of its value each year.
How many years will it be before the system is worth less than £20 000?

19 The population of Ashton has increased by 5.5% a year for the last 5 years.
The present population of Ashton is 20 000.
Find how many years it will be before the population has grown by a quarter.

> 'To grow by a quarter' means add on a quarter of the present size.

20 A new town of 3000 houses is built.
The plan is to increase the number of houses by 15% next year, 10% the year after and 5% in the following year.
How many houses need to be built in these three years?

21 A pest eradication scheme aims to reduce the number of mice in a grain store by 20% a month.
At the beginning of October it is estimated that there are 20 000 mice.
How many months will it take to at least halve the number of mice?

22 Radioactive materials decay with time.
One radioactive material loses 10% of its mass each year.
How long will it take 1 kg of this material to reduce its mass to below 700 grams?

23 Rob puts £5000 in a savings account.
He gets interest of 4% p.a. which he withdraws each year.
Work out how much more interest he would get over 3 years if he did not take the interest out each year.

A01 **24** Sally invests £10 000 in a business.
Her investment increases by 10% a year for each of the first three years and then decreases in value by 30% in the fourth year.
Her brother George invests £10 000 in a different business.
His investment loses 30% in the first year and then increases in value by 10% a year for the next three years.
Whose investment is worth more after 4 years?
Give reasons for your answer.

Summary of key points

- You can express a percentage as a fraction or as a decimal by writing it as a fraction with denominator 100. Dividing the top by the bottom gives a decimal, and simplifying gives a fraction in its lowest terms.
- You can express a fraction or a decimal as a percentage by multiplying it by 100 and adding a percentage sign.
- You find a percentage of a quantity by multiplying the quantity by the percentage written as a fraction or a decimal.
- You find one quantity as a percentage of another by putting the first quantity over the second and multiplying by 100 (make sure that both quantities are in the same units).
- A percentage increase or decrease is always a percentage of the quantity before it is changed.
- A multiplier is a number used to increase or decrease a quantity.
  The multiplier to increase by 8% is 1.08.
  The multiplier to decrease by 8% is 0.92.
- You can find the original quantity by dividing the final value by the multiplier that changed it.
- You need to read percentage questions carefully to make sure that you know what you are being asked to find.

Most candidates who get GRADE C or above can:
- calculate a percentage increase or decrease
- find a compound percentage change.

Glossary

Compound interest	interest that is left in an account, so the amount increases year by year
Denominator	the bottom number in a fraction
Interest	money that is paid (or charged) by banks on money in an account (or money that is borrowed)
Multiplier	a number that is multiplied by a quantity to increase or decrease the quantity
Percent	each hundred, so 12% means $\frac{12}{10}$
Simple interest	interest that is paid on the same amount each year
VAT	value added tax, which is a tax that is added to most items that are sold

9 Algebra and graphs

9.1 Formulae, expressions and equations

Algebra is a part of mathematics in which letters are used to represent unknown numbers or quantities, or numbers that can vary.

A **formula** is a rule connecting quantities.
The rule for finding the area of a rectangle is a formula.
Using the letters A for the area, l for the length and b for the breadth, the formula can be written using algebra as $A = l \times b$.
The area, length and breadth can vary. The letters A, l and b are called **variables**.

> The area of a rectangle = length × breadth.

An **expression** is any collection of letters and numbers without an equals sign.

> $l \times b$ is an expression.

An **equation** always has an equals sign. Usually two expressions are equal for only some values of the letters.

> 3 is the only value of x for which $x + 2 = 5$.

When the two expressions are equal for any values of the letters, it is called an **identity**.

> Two numbers can be added in any order. So $a + b = b + a$ is an identity because it is true for any two numbers.

9.2 Simplifying expressions

Simplifying an expression means writing it in as short a form as possible.

When you multiply letters you can leave out the multiplication sign.

You can also use indices when a letter is multiplied by itself.

So $q \times q \times q$ can be written as q^3.

> $2a$ means $2 \times a$,
> $3pq$ means $3 \times p \times q$,
> $5x^2$ means $5 \times x \times x$.
> It is convention to write the number first, then the letters in alphabetical order e.g. $3ab$ rather than $b3a$.

Example 1

Simplify: **a** $2p \times 5q$ **b** $3b \times 4b^2$

a $2p \times 5q = 2 \times p \times 5 \times q$
$= 2 \times 5 \times p \times q$
$= 10 \times pq$
$= 10pq$

> Because the letters represent numbers, the ordinary rules of arithmetic apply. So you can change the order of the multiplication.

b $3b \times 4b^2 = 3 \times b \times 4 \times b \times b$
$= 3 \times 4 \times b \times b \times b$
$= 12b^3$

> There is no need to write down all this working. If you are confident, go straight to the simplified form.

A **term** in an expression is any collection of numbers and letters that are not separated by plus or minus signs.
So the terms in the expression $2y^2 - 3y + 5$ are $2y^2$, $3y$ and 5.

> A term that is just a number, such as 5, is called a **constant**.

Like terms contain exactly the same combination of letters.
So x and $3x$ are like terms but x and x^2 are not.

> Like terms can have different numbers in them but they must have exactly the same combination of letters.

Like terms can be added or subtracted to give a single term.
So $3x + 5x$ can be simplified to $8x$.
This is called collecting like terms.

> $3x$ mean $x + x + x$ and $5x$ means $x + x + x + x + x$.
> Adding them gives 8 lots of x, or $8x$.

Example 2

Simplify: **a** $5pq - 2qp$ **b** $x^2 - 2x + 5 - x$ **c** $\sqrt{5} + \sqrt{20}$

a $5pq - 2qp = 3pq$

> The order in which you multiply does not matter, so $2qp = 2pq$. So $2qp$ and $5pq$ and are like terms.

b $x^2 - 2x + 5 - x = x^2 - 2x - x + 5$
$= x^2 - 3x + 5$

> The ordinary rules of arithmetic apply so you can rearrange the expression so that the like terms are together.

c $\sqrt{5} + \sqrt{20} = \sqrt{5} + \sqrt{4 \times 5} = \sqrt{5} + \sqrt{4} \times \sqrt{5} = \sqrt{5} + 2\sqrt{5} = 3\sqrt{5}$

> $\sqrt{5}$ and $2\sqrt{5}$ can be treated as like terms and simplified.

Exam practice 9A

1 Simplify:
  a $3a \times 5a$ **b** $3p \times 5p$ **c** $2x \times 4y$
  d $5b \times 6$ **e** $4 \times 3x$ **f** $3s^2 \times 2t$
  g $2a^2 \times 3b \times a$ **h** $(-3a) \times (-2)$ **i** $(-2t) \times 5t$
  j $(-5t) \times (-3s)$ **k** $2 \times (-2a) \times (-2b)$ **l** $(-3x) \times 4 \times (-2y)$

> Remember that the product of two negative numbers is positive. The product of a negative number and a positive number is negative.

2 Simplify:
- **a** $2x + x + x$
- **b** $3x - 2x + x$
- **c** $-4x + 10x - 2x$
- **d** $6 + 2a - 3a$
- **e** $7x + x + 13 - 8$
- **f** $3x - y + 2x + 2y$
- **g** $9p - 6 + 3p$
- **h** $4a - 2b - 7a - 4b$
- **i** $-2x + 5 - 3x - 1$

3 Simplify:
- **a** $x^2 + 6x + 2x$
- **b** $a^2 + 2a + a + 3$
- **c** $2a^2 + 6a - 8a + 9$
- **d** $x^2 - xy + 3xy - 2$
- **e** $5p^2 - 2p + 6 + 4p$
- **f** $3y - y^2 - 2y + 7$
- **g** $7x^2 - 3x - 7x + 4$
- **h** $a^2 - 2a - 9a + 8$
- **i** $4t^2 - 3t + 8 - 5t$

4 Simplify:
- **a** $\sqrt{3} + \sqrt{48}$
- **b** $\sqrt{2} + \sqrt{18}$
- **c** $\sqrt{3} + \sqrt{12}$
- **d** $\sqrt{18} + 4\sqrt{2}$
- **e** $7\sqrt{3} - \sqrt{27}$
- **f** $\sqrt{48} - 2\sqrt{12}$
- **g** $\sqrt{98} - \sqrt{50}$
- **h** $2\sqrt{48} - \sqrt{75}$

9.3 Multiplying out brackets

The expression $3(2x - 7)$ means 3 multiplied by each term inside the bracket. So $3(2x - 7) = 3 \times 2x - 3 \times 7 = 6x - 21$
This process is called **multiplying out** the bracket.

> Multiplying out a bracket is sometimes called **expanding the bracket**.

Example 3

Multiply out and simplify $5(x - 2) - x(2x - 4)$.

$$5(x - 2) - x(2x - 4) = 5x - 10 - 2x^2 + 4x$$
$$= 9x - 10 - 2x^2$$

> Expand each bracket. Remember that $-x \times -4 = +4x$. Collect like terms.

The expression $(2x - 5)(x + 4)$ means each term in the second bracket is multiplied by each term in the first bracket.
So $(2x - 5)(x + 4) = 2x(x + 4) - 5(x + 4)$
$$= 2x^2 + 8x - 5x - 20$$
$$= 2x^2 + 3x - 20$$

> You can use a grid like this:
>
> | | x | 4 |
> |-----|--------|-------|
> | $2x$ | $2x^2$ | $8x$ |
> | -5 | $-5x$ | -20 |

Example 4

Multiply out and simplify $(3x - 2)(2x - 5)$.

$$(3x - 2)(2x - 5) = 3x(2x - 5) - 2(2x - 5)$$
$$= 6x^2 - 15x - 4x + 10$$
$$= 6x^2 - 19x + 10$$

> If you are confident you can leave out the second step.

Expressions containing surds and brackets can often be simplified by multiplying out the brackets.

Example 5

Express $(2 - 3\sqrt{2})^2$ in the form $p - q\sqrt{2}$ where p and q are integers.

$$
\begin{aligned}
(2 - 3\sqrt{2})^2 &= (2 - 3\sqrt{2})(2 - 3\sqrt{2}) \\
&= 2(2 - 3\sqrt{2}) - 3\sqrt{2}(2 - 3\sqrt{2}) \\
&= 4 - 6\sqrt{2} - 6\sqrt{2} + 18 \\
&= 22 - 12\sqrt{2}
\end{aligned}
$$

$(2 - 3\sqrt{2})^2$ means $(2 - 3\sqrt{2})$ multiplied by itself.

Multiply out the brackets and remember that $\sqrt{2} \times \sqrt{2} = 2$ so $3\sqrt{2} \times 3\sqrt{2} = 3 \times 3 \times \sqrt{2} \times \sqrt{2} = 9 \times 2$

Example 6

Show that $(2\sqrt{18} - 3\sqrt{2})^2 = 18$.

$$
\begin{aligned}
(2\sqrt{18} - 3\sqrt{2})^2 &= (2\sqrt{18} - 3\sqrt{2})(2\sqrt{18} - 3\sqrt{2}) \\
&= 2\sqrt{18}(2\sqrt{18} - 3\sqrt{2}) - 3\sqrt{2}(2\sqrt{18} - 3\sqrt{2}) \\
&= 4 \times 18 - 6 \times \sqrt{36} - 6\sqrt{36} + 9 \times 2 \\
&= 4 \times 18 - 6 \times 6 - 6 \times 6 + 9 \times 2 \\
&= 72 - 36 - 36 + 18 \\
&= 18
\end{aligned}
$$

Alternatively:
$$
\begin{aligned}
(2\sqrt{18} - 3\sqrt{2})^2 \\
= (2\sqrt{9 \times 2} - 3\sqrt{2})^2 \\
= (2\sqrt{9} \times \sqrt{2} - 3\sqrt{2})^2 \\
= (6\sqrt{2} - 3\sqrt{2})^2 \\
= (3\sqrt{2})^2 \\
= 9 \times 2 \\
= 18
\end{aligned}
$$

Exam practice 9B

1 Multiply out and simplify:

a $2(5 - 3x)$ b $4y(7 - 3y)$

c $2pq(3p - 2q)$ d $3(3 - a) - a(5 - 2a)$

e $3x(x - 3) - 2(4 - x)$ f $2(x - 5y) + 4(x + y)$

g $x(x - y) + 2y(x + 3y)$ h $6(x - 2y) - (x + y)$

i $x(2 - x) - (4 - 3x)$

$-(x + y)$ means the same as $-1(x + y)$.

2 Multiply out and simplify:

a $(x - 4)(2x + 1)$ b $(2a - 7)(3 - 5a)$ c $(2x + 3)(5x + 4)$

d $(2s - t)(3s + 2t)$ e $(7y + 3)(2y + 9)$ f $(4t - 1)(t - 3)$

g $(x - 2)(x + 2)$ h $(3x + 1)(3x - 1)$ i $(2 - y)(5 - 2y)$

j $(x + 3)^2$ k $(x - 5)^2$ l $(2x + 1)^2$

m $(3x - 1)^2$ n $(2x + 3)^2$ p $(4 - 3x)^2$

3 Multiply out and simplify:

a $\sqrt{2}(1 - \sqrt{2})$ b $(1 + \sqrt{2})^2$

c $(1 + \sqrt{2})(1 - \sqrt{2})$ d $(1 - \sqrt{2})^2$

e $\sqrt{5}(2\sqrt{5} - 3)$ f $5\sqrt{3}(4 - \sqrt{3})$

g $\sqrt{3}(\sqrt{2} - \sqrt{3})$ h $(2\sqrt{3} - 1)^2$

i $(\sqrt{3} - 2\sqrt{27})(2\sqrt{3} + \sqrt{27})$

4 Show that $3\sqrt{2}(\sqrt{18} - \sqrt{8}) = 6$.

5 Multiply out $(2 + \sqrt{3})(3 - \sqrt{2})$.

6 Simplify $(\sqrt{5} - 2\sqrt{15})(\sqrt{5} + \sqrt{15})$.
Give your answer in the form $p + q\sqrt{3}$ where p and q are integers.

7 Show that $(\sqrt{18} + \sqrt{8})(\sqrt{18} - \sqrt{8}) = 10$.

8 Show that $(\sqrt{2} + 2\sqrt{6})(\sqrt{2} - \sqrt{6}) = a + b\sqrt{3}$ where a and b are integers. Give the values of a and b.

9 **a** Multiply the top and bottom of the fraction $\dfrac{1}{\sqrt{2} - 1}$ by $\sqrt{2} + 1$.

  b Use your answer to part **a** show that $= \dfrac{1}{\sqrt{2} - 1} = \sqrt{2} + 1$.

9.4 Proof

You can show that a statement is not true by finding an example that contradicts it. This is called a **counter example**.

You cannot use an example to prove that a statement is true. An example is a demonstration that the statement is true for that example. It may not be true for other examples.
To prove a statement you need to show that it is true for all possible examples. Variables are useful for **proofs** because they can stand for any possible number.

Example 7

True or false?
a The sum of any two odd numbers is odd.
b The sum of any two odd numbers is even.

a 3 and 5 are odd numbers and $3 + 5 = 8$ which is an even number.

So it is not true that the sum of any two odd numbers is odd.

> $3 + 5 = 8$ is the counter example.

b $2n + 1$ and $2m + 1$ are any two odd numbers when n and m are any two integers.

$(2n + 1) + (2m + 1) = 2n + 2m + 2 = 2(n + m + 1)$

This is the sum of two odd numbers.

> You can write any odd number as $2n + 1$ where n is an integer.

$2(n + m + 1)$ is an even number because it divides exactly by 2.
This proves that the statement is true for any two odd numbers.

Exam practice 9C

1 Find a counter example to show that it is not true that $x^2 > x$ for any number x.

Do not assume that the number is an integer.

2 Prove that the sum of any three consecutive natural numbers is a multiple of 3.

Use n for the first number. The second number is $n + 1$, and so on.

3 Find a counter example to show that it is not true that the sum of any two prime numbers is even.

4 Prove that the square of an odd number is also an odd number.

Start with $2n + 1$. To prove that a number is odd you have to show it will not divide by 2.

5 Prove that the square of an even number is a multiple of 4.

6 Prove that the product of two odd numbers is an odd number.

9.5 Drawing graphs

Equations can be represented graphically.

Any equation of the form $y = mx + c$ produces a straight line graph where m and c are constants. These equations are called **linear equations**.

$y = 3x - 2$ is a linear equation.
$m = 3$ and $c = -2$.

You may have to rearrange an equation such as $2y - 3x = -2$ to make it look like $y = mx + c$.
You can rearrange any equation by
- adding or subtracting the same quantity from both sides
- multiplying or dividing both sides by the same quantity.

Example 8

Draw the graph of $2y - 3x = -2$ for values of x between -2 and 3.

$2y - 3x = -2$

$2y = 3x - 2$ Add $3x$ to both sides.

$y = 1.5x - 1$ Divide both sides by 2

x	-2	0	2
y	-4	-1	2

$x = -2$ so
$y = 1.5 \times (-2) - 1$
$= -3 - 1 = -4.$

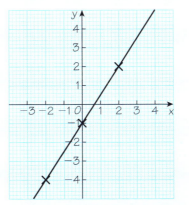

Rearrange the equation to look like $y = mx + c$.

Make a table of values for different values of x.
To draw a straight line you only need two points. Find three points to check your working.

Find the value of y for each value of x and plot these points on a coordinate grid. Join your points with a straight line.

Equations of the form $y = ax^2 - bx + c$ where a, b and c are constants are called **quadratic equations**.

> $y = 2x^2 - 3$ is a quadratic equation. $a = 2$, $b = 0$ and $c = -3$.

When a graph of a quadratic equation is drawn it gives a curve called a **parabola**.

Example 9

a Draw the graph of $y = 2x^2 - 3$ for values of x from -2 to 2.

b Use your graph to find the approximate values of x when $y = 3$.

a

x	-2	-1	$-\frac{1}{2}$	0	$\frac{1}{2}$	1	2
$2x^2$	8	2	$\frac{1}{2}$	0	$\frac{1}{2}$	2	8
$y = 2x^2 - 3$	5	-1	-2.5	-3	-2.5	-1	5

> Make a table of values.
> Start with integer values of x. You will need other values near the point where the graph turns.
> To find y when $x = -2$, replace x in $2x^2 - 3$ with -2:
> $2(-2)^2 - 3 = 8 - 3$.
> You may find it helps to add extra rows to the table.

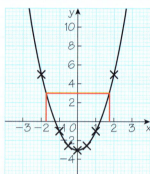

> Plot the points and draw a smooth curve through them.

b $x = -1.7$ and 1.7

> Draw a horizontal line at $y = 3$ to the graph then go down to the x-axis and read the values of x. These values are approximate because you cannot always read values accurately from a graph.

All graphs of quadratic equations look like 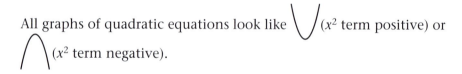 (x^2 term positive) or (x^2 term negative).

Exam practice 9D

1 Copy and complete this table of values for the equation $y + 3x = 4$.

x	-2	0	4
y		4	

2 a Use a copy of this grid to draw the graphs of
    i $y = x + 1$ ii $y = 4x + 1$
    iii $y = 3 - 2x$ iv $y = 1 - x$
  b Write down the coordinates of the point where the lines $y = x + 1$ and $y = 3 - 2x$ cross.

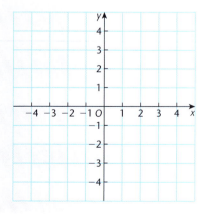

3 Rearrange these equations so that they are in the form $y = mx + c$.
   a $y - 2x = 3$ b $4y - 5x = 12$ c $5y + 7x = -10$
   d $3y + 6x = 2$ e $y - x + 2 = 0$ f $2x - 3y - 2 = 0$

4 a Draw the graphs of $y + x = 2$ and $4x + 2y - 3 = 0$ on the same set of axes for values of x between -2 and 4.
   b Write down the coordinates of the point where the two lines cross.

5 Copy and complete this table of values for the equation $y = 2x^2 - 2x + 5$.

x	-4	-2	-1	0	1	2	4
y	45			5			29

6 a Copy and complete this table of values for the equation $y = 2x^2 + 6x$.

x	-4	-3	-2	-1.5	-1	0	1
y	8		-4			0	

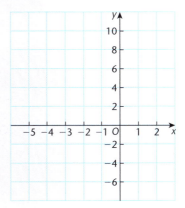

   b Use the values in your table to draw the graph of $y = 2x^2 + 6x$.
     Use a grid like this.
   c Write down the values of x when
     i $y = 2$ ii $y = -3$.
   d What is the least value of y?

7 a Copy and complete this table of values for the equation $y = 3x - x^2$.

x	-1	0	1	1.5	2	3	4
y		0			2		-4

   b Draw the graph of $y = 3x - x^2$ for these values of x.
   c Write down the values of x when $y = -1$.
   d i What is the maximum value of y?
     ii What is the value of x where y has its maximum value?

> Maximum value means biggest value. Minimum value means smallest value.
>
> Start by finding values of y for integer values of x. This will show you roughly where the graph turns. Add more values of x close to this point.

8 a Draw the graph of $y = x^2 - 6x + 2$ for values of x from -1 to 7.
   b Write down the value of x where y has its minimum value.

9.6 Using graphs to solve equations

Solving an equation means finding the value or values of the letters that make both sides of the equation equal.
So the solution of the equation $x + 4 = 6$ is $x = 2$.

The equation $x + 4 = 6$ is an example of a linear equation in one unknown. Equations like this have only one solution.

The equation $y = 3x - 2$ is a linear equation in two unknowns. It has many solutions: $x = 1$ and $y = 1$ is just one of them.

> You can also say that $x = 2$ satisfies the equation $x + 4 = 6$.
> 2 is called the **root** of the equation.

Simultaneous linear equations

There is often one solution that satisfies two linear equations. This solution can be found by drawing graphs.

> When two equations have solutions in common, they are called simultaneous equations. **Simultaneous** means occurring at the same time.

Example 10

This diagram shows the graphs of $y = 2x - 3$ and $y = 6x - 4$.
Use the graph to find the solution of the simultaneous equations
$y = 2x - 3$ and $y = 6x - 4$.

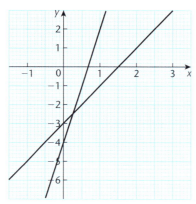

> The value of x and of y that satisfies both equations will be the coordinates of the point that is on both lines. This is where the lines cross or **intersect**.

The point of intersection is $(0.25, -2.5)$.
The solution is $x = 0.25$ and $y = -2.5$.

> You can usually read values from a graph to at most 2 decimal places.

Quadratic equations

The equation $y = 2x^2 - 3x$ is a quadratic equation in two unknowns. The equation $2x^2 - 3x = 4$ is an example of a quadratic equation in one unknown. Equations like this usually have two solutions or roots.
You can find approximate values of these roots from a graph.

Example 11

This is the graph of $y = x^2 - 3x - 1$.

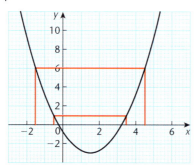

Use the graph to find approximate values of the roots of the equation
a $x^2 - 3x - 1 = 1$ **b** $x^2 - 3x - 7 = 0$.

a   When $y = 1$, $x \simeq -0.6$ or 3.6

so the roots of the equation $x^2 - 3x - 1 = 1$ are

approximately -0.6 and 3.6.

> $x^2 - 3x - 1 = 1$ when $y = 1$.
> The roots are the x-values at the intersections of the curve $y = x^2 - 3x - 1$ and the line $y = 1$. Read the values as accurately as you can. For this graph this is correct to 1 d.p.

b $x^2 - 3x - 7 = 0$

$x^2 - 3x - 1 = 6$

when $y = 6$, $x \simeq -1.5$ or 4.5

so the roots of the equation $x^2 - 3x - 7 = 0$ are

approximately -1.5 and 4.5.

> To use the graph of $y = x^2 - 3x - 1$, you need to rearrange $x^2 - 3x - 7 = 0$ so that the left-hand side is $x^2 - 3x - 1$. You do this by adding 6 to both sides.

Exam practice 9E

WWW

1   This is the graph of $y = 3x - 4$.

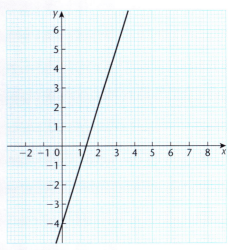

a   Copy the graph and add the graph of $y + x = 5$.

b   Use your graphs to find the solution of the simultaneous equations $y = 3x - 4$ and $y + x = 5$.

2   a   Draw the graphs of $y = x + 1$ and $y = 3x - 2$ on the same axes for values of x from -2 to 4.
    b   Use your graph to solve the equations simultaneously.

3   Rearrange each of the following equations so that the left-hand side is equal to $x^2 - 3x + 5$.
    a $x^2 - 3x + 6 = 0$ b $x^2 - 3x - 2 = 0$ c $x^2 - 3x - 10 = 0$

4   This is the graph of $y = x^2 - 3x + 5$.

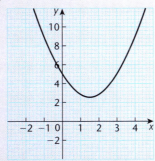

a   Use the graph to find the approximate solutions to the equation $x^2 - 3x - 2 = 0$.

A01

b   Explain why the equation $x^2 - 3x + 5 = 0$ has no solution.

5 This is the graph of $y = x^2 + x - 5$.

Use the graph to find approximate values for the roots of the following equations:

a $x^2 + x - 5 = 0$

b $x^2 + x - 5 = 1$

c $x^2 + x - 7 = 0$

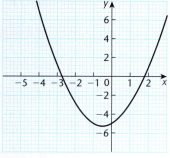

6 Draw the graph of $y = 2x^2 - 4x + 1$ for values of x from -1 to 3. Use the graph to find the solutions of the equations:

a $2x^2 - 4x + 1 = 0$

b $2x^2 - 4x - 1 = 0$

c $2x^2 - 4x = 0$

9.7 Simultaneous equations, one linear and one quadratic

Simultaneous equations containing one quadratic equation and one linear equation can have two solutions. The solutions can be found by drawing graphs and finding their points of intersection.

Example 12

Draw the graphs of $y = 2x^2 - 3x + 1$ and $2y = 4 - 3x$ for values of x between $x = -1$ and $x = 2$.
Use your graph to find the solutions of the simultaneous equations $y = 2x^2 - 3x + 1$ and $2y = 4 - 3x$.

$y = 2x^2 - 3x + 1$

x	−1	0	0.5	0.75	1	1.5	2
y	6	1	0	−0.125	0	1	3

The symbol ⇒ means 'gives'.

$2y = 4 - 3x \Rightarrow y = 2 - 1.5x$

$y = 2 - 1.5x$

x	−1	0	1
y	3.5	2	0.5

Write $2y = 4 - 3x$ in the form $y = mx + c$. You do this by dividing both sides by 2.

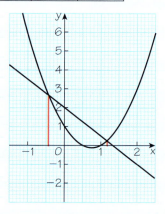

The coordinates of the points of intersection are $(-0.4, 2.6)$ and $(1.2, 0.2)$.

The solutions are $x = -0.4$, $y = 2.6$ and $x = 1.2$, $y = 0.2$.

The values of x and y that satisfy both equations are the coordinates of the points where the graphs intersect.

This idea can be used to solve any quadratic equation from any quadratic graph.

You do this by rearranging the quadratic equation so that the left-hand side is the same as the equation of the quadratic graph.

Example 13

This is the graph of $y = x^2 - 4$.
By drawing a suitable linear graph find the solutions of $x^2 - x - 3 = 0$.

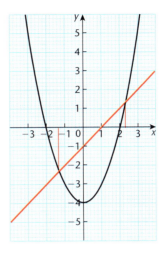

$x^2 - x - 3 = 0 \Rightarrow x^2 - x + x - 3 - 1 = x - 1$
$\qquad\qquad\qquad \Rightarrow x^2 - 4 = x - 1$

The graph is for $y = x^2 - 4$, so rearrange $x^2 - x - 3 = 0$ so that the left-hand side is equal to $x^2 - 4$.

x	-1	0	1
$y = x - 1$	-2	-1	0

Draw the graph of $y = x - 1$.

$x = 2.3$ or -1.3.

The graphs $y = x^2 - 4$ and $y = x - 1$ intersect where $x^2 - 4 = x - 1$, so the values of x at these points give the solution to the equation $x^2 - 4 = x - 1$. These are the solutions of the equation $x^2 - x - 3 = 0$.

Exam practice 9F

1 This is the graph of $y = 2x^2 + 8x - 5$.

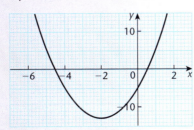

　a On a copy of this graph, draw the line needed to solve the simultaneous equations
　　　$y = 2x^2 + 8x - 5$ and $y = 3x - 2$.
　b Write down the solutions.

2 Using values of x from -5 to 2, draw graphs to find the solutions of the simultaneous equations
　　　$y = 2x^2 + 4x - 1$ and $x - 3y + 1 = 0$.

Remember you need more values near where the graph turns.

3 Rearrange each equation so that the left-hand side is equal to
   $x^2 + x$.
   a $x^2 + x - 3 = 0$ b $x^2 - x = 0$
   c $x^2 - x - 4 = 0$ d $x^2 - 2x + 4$

4 Rearrange each equation so that the left-hand side is equal to
   $x^2 + 5x - 6$.
   a $x^2 - x + 1 = 0$ b $x^2 + x - 2 = 0$
   c $x^2 + 2x + 6 = 0$ d $x^2 + 8x + 4 = 0$

5 Explain how you would use the graph of $y = x^2 + 7x - 2$ to solve
   these equations:
   a $x^2 + x = 0$ b $(x - 2)(x + 4) = 3$
   c $5 - x^2 = 0$ d $2x^2 + 14x - 10 = 0$

www 6 This is the graph of $y = x^2 - 4x - 9$.

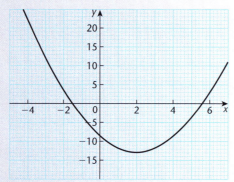

   On a copy of the graph, draw the appropriate line to solve the
   equation $x^2 - x - 13 = 0$.

www 7 This is the graph of $y = 10 - x^2$.

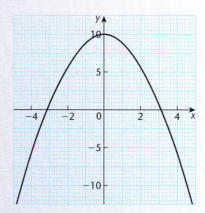

   a Copy the graph and use it to solve the equation $10 - x^2 = 0$.
   b Draw the graph of $y = 2x + 5$ on the same axes.
   c Write down
      i   the values of x at the points of intersection of the two
          graphs
      ii the equation that has these values of x as roots.

Summary of key points

- Letters are used to represent numbers or quantities that are unknown or can vary.
- Expressions can be simplified by multiplying out brackets and collecting like terms.
- The graph of a linear equation, such as $y = 5x + 7$, is a straight line.
- The graph of a quadratic equation, such as $y = 3x^2 - 2x + 4$, is shaped $\bigvee$ or $\bigwedge$.
- Quadratic equations in one unknown usually have two solutions which you can find by drawing a quadratic graph and an appropriate straight line.
- Simultaneous equations can be solved by finding the point where the graphs intersect.

Most candidates who get GRADE C or above can:

- multiply out brackets
- draw linear and quadratic graphs.

Most candidates who get GRADE A or above can also:

- simplify expressions containing surds and brackets
- solve a quadratic and linear equation simultaneously using graphs
- find and draw the appropriate linear graph together with the graph of a quadratic equation in order to solve another quadratic equation.

Glossary

Constant	a fixed value
Counter example	a demonstration showing that a statement is false
Equation	two expressions that are equal
Expanding brackets	multiplying out brackets
Expression	a collection of numbers and letters with no equals sign
Formula	a rule
Identity	an equation which is true for all values of the variables
Intersect	cross or cut or touch
Like terms	terms with exactly the same combination of letters
Linear equation	equation of a straight line
Multiply out	multiply each term inside a bracket by the term the bracket is multiplied by
Parabola	the shape of the graph of a quadratic equation
Perfect square	a number or expression that can be written as the product of two equal factors
Proof	an argument that shows a statement is true in all possible cases
Quadratic equation	equation containing x^2 and no higher powers of x
Root	a number that satisfies an equation
Simultaneous	occurring at the same time
Term	a collection of numbers and letters that are not separated by plus or minus signs
Variable	a letter representing a quantity or number that can have varying values

10 Ratio and proportion

This chapter will show you:
- ✓ the meaning of ratio
- ✓ the relationship between ratios and fractions
- ✓ how to divide a quantity in a given ratio
- ✓ how to work with quantities that are directly proportional
- ✓ how to work with quantities that are inversely proportional
- ✓ how to write equations for direct and inverse proportion

Before you start you need to know:
- ✓ how to simplify fractions
- ✓ how to find a fraction of a quantity
- ✓ the meaning of significant figures
- ✓ units of length, mass and capacity
- ✓ the units used to describe area and volume
- ✓ that letters can be used to represent quantities
- ✓ how to solve simple equations
- ✓ how to use a multiplier (sometimes called a scale factor)

10.1 Ratio

Ratio is a way of comparing quantities.

The label on a bottle of squash says 'Mix 1 part of squash with 4 parts of water.'

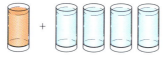

This compares the quantities of squash and water needed to make a drink.

It is called the **ratio** of the amount of squash to the amount of water.
You can write this as 'the ratio of squash to water is 1 to 4'
or simply as   squash : water = 1 : 4.

The **symbol ':'** means 'to'.

Class discussion
Why do you think there are no units in a ratio?

Simplifying ratios

Ratios are easier to work with when the numbers are as small as possible. Simplifying ratios is very similar to simplifying fractions.

Example 1

Write this instruction as a ratio in its simplest terms:
   'Mix 200 ml of syrup with 500 ml of water'.

$$\text{Syrup : water} = 200\,\text{ml} : 500\,\text{ml}$$
$$= 200 : 500$$
$$= 2 : 5$$

You can simplify the ratio 200 ml : 500 ml by leaving out the units.
You can always leave out the units as long as they are the same for both quantities.

You can simplify 200 : 500 by dividing both parts by 100.

When you simplify ratios you must make sure that both quantities are in the same units.

Example 2

Simplify the ratio 2 m : 30 cm.

2 m : 30 cm = 200 cm : 30 cm
= 200 : 30
= 20 : 3

> You must write both lengths in the same units before simplifying.

You can use ratios to compare more than two quantities.

Example 3

Find the ratio of the lengths of the sides of this triangle.

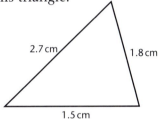

2.7 cm   1.8 cm
1.5 cm

Ratio of the lengths = 2.7 cm : 1.8 cm : 1.5 cm
= 2.7 : 1.8 : 1.5 — The units are the same so you can remove them.
= 27 : 18 : 15 — Multiply by 10 to make them all whole numbers.
= 9 : 6 : 5 — Divide each number by 3 to simplify the ratio.

Expressing a ratio in the form 1: *n*

Ratios are sometimes given with the first part as 1, even though the second part is not a whole number.
You can write any ratio in this form. It is useful when finding the second quantity.
1 : *n* = first quantity : second quantity
So the second quantity can be found by using the multiplier *n*.

> The ratio 20 : 55 can be written as 1 : 2.75 by dividing both parts by 20.

Example 4

Express 2 : 5 in the form 1 : *n*.

2 : 5 = (2 ÷ 2) : (5 ÷ 2)
= 1 : 2.5

> To make the first number in this ratio 1, you need to divide both numbers by 2.

Exam practice 10A

1 Simplify the following ratios:

   a   3 cm : 12 cm   **b**   £8 : £1.50   **c**   16 mm : 4 mm

   d   13 m : 39 m   **e**   45p : £2.70   **f**   1.50 kg : 750 g

   g   2 m : $1\frac{1}{2}$ m   **h**   0.8 m : 1.6 m   **i** $1\frac{1}{2}$ oz : $1\frac{1}{4}$ oz

2 Simplify the following ratios:

   a   3 cl : 6 cl : 9 cl   **b**   20 g : 80 g : 60 g

   c   24 mg : 42 mg : 18 mg   **d**   2 kg : 400 g : 500 mg

   e $2\frac{1}{2}$ lb : 3 lb : $1\frac{1}{2}$ lb

   f   30 seconds : $1\frac{1}{2}$ minutes : 5 minutes

> 1 mg = 0.001 g

3 Square A has sides 12 cm long and square B has sides 16 cm long.
   Find the ratio of the length of the side of square A to the length of the side of square B.

> Make sure that the numbers in the ratio are in the same order as the words. For this question you need the length for A first.

4 There are 12 boys and 8 girls in a playground.

   a   Find the ratio of the number of boys to the number of girls.

   b   Find the ratio of the number of girls to the number of children.

> Read the question carefully. Make sure you understand which quantities you need.

5 A triangle has sides of lengths 3.2 cm, 4.8 cm and 3.6 cm.
   Find the ratio of the lengths of the sides.

6 David runs his own business.

   a   Last year his costs were £25 000 and his turnover was £40 000.
       Find the ratio of his costs to turnover last year.

   b   This year his costs have increased by 10% and his turnover has fallen by 5%.
       Find the ratio of his costs to turnover this year.

7 Express the ratio 5 cm to 4 metres in the form 1 : n.

> First simplify the ratio. Then divide both numbers by the first number.

8 Express the ratio 20 ml to 30 cl as a ratio in the form 1 : n.

9 A road that is 12 km long is shown by a line on a map that is 4 cm long.
   Find the ratio of the length of the line on the map to the length of the road. Give your answer in the form 1 : n.

10 A 50 ml bottle of liquid plant food dilutes to give 10 litres of spray.
   Find the ratio of liquid food to spray.
   Give your answer in the form 1 : n.

10.2 Ratios and fractions

Ratios and fractions are closely related.

The ratio
  1 part of squash : 4 parts of water
tells you that squash is $\frac{1}{4}$ of the amount
of water and $\frac{1}{5}$ of the fruit drink.

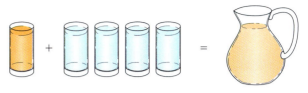

You can use fractions to find one quantity when you know the size of
the other quantity and the ratio of the two quantities.

Example 5

Concentrated fabric conditioner is diluted with water in the ratio
1 : 5.
How much conditioner should be added to 2 litres of water?

Conditioner : water = 1 : 5

So conditioner = $\frac{1}{5}$ of the water

2000 ÷ 5 = 400

400 ml of conditioner is needed.

So $\frac{1}{5}$ of 2 litres of
water is needed.
2 litres = 2000 ml.

Example 6

Ken read 'To make a potting compost mix 2 parts of sand with 3 parts
of earth.'
How much sand does Ken need to mix with 7 buckets of earth?

Sand : earth = 2 : 3

So the amount of sand is $\frac{2}{3}$ the amount of earth.

Ken needs $\frac{2}{3}$ of 7 buckets of sand.

$\frac{2}{3} \times 7 = 2 \times 7 \div 3 = 14 \div 3 = 4\frac{2}{3}$

Ken needs $4\frac{2}{3}$ buckets of sand.

The instructions tell Ken that sand
and earth are mixed in the ratio
  2 parts sand : 3 parts earth
  − 2 : 3 − $\frac{2}{3}$: 1
Ken needs $\frac{2}{3} \times 7$ buckets of sand.

Exam practice 10B

1 Jan has 42 cm of ribbon.
   She needs lengths of elastic and ribbon in the ratio 3 : 7
   to make a hair band.
   Work out the length of elastic she needs.

   Start by writing down the
   length of the elastic as a fraction
   of the length of the ribbon.

2 The ratio of the width to the length of this rectangle is 4 : 9.
   Find the length of the rectangle.

32 cm

3 A model of a building is 12 cm high.
   The ratio of the height of the actual building to the height of the model is 200 : 1.
   How high is the building?

4 The ratio of the cost of a basic computer to the cost of the software needed is 3 : 2.
   The cost of a basic computer is £380.
   Work out the cost of the software.

5 A photograph is enlarged so that the ratio of the length of the enlargement to the length of the original is 5 : 2.
   The original photo is 15 cm long.
   What is the length of the enlarged photo?

6 The ratio of boys to girls doing a catering course is 2 : 5.
   There are 20 girls on the course.
   How many boys are on the course?

7 A lemon drink is made by mixing fresh lemon juice and water in the ratio 2 : 3.
   a How many cupfuls of water are needed to mix with half a cupful of lemon juice?
   b Work out the quantity of lemon juice needed to mix with 500 ml of water.

8 Concrete is made by mixing cement, sand and aggregate in the ratio 3 : 4 : 8.
   a How much aggregate should be mixed with 20 kg of sand?
   b Find how much cement is needed for 500 kg of aggregate.

10.3 Dividing in a given ratio

When you know the size of a quantity made by combining two or more quantities in a given ratio, you can find the size of each part.

When squash and water are mixed in the ratio 1 : 4, you can see that squash is $\frac{1}{5}$ of the mixture and water is $\frac{4}{5}$ of the mixture. So in 2 litres of mixture there is

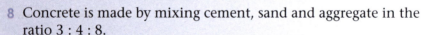

$\frac{1}{5}$ of 2 litres of squash = $\frac{1}{5}$ × 2000 ml = 2000 ÷ 5 ml = 400 ml

and $\frac{4}{5}$ of 2 litres of water = 4 × 2000 ÷ 5 ml = 1600 ml

So there is 400 ml of squash and 1600 ml of water.

> You can check your answer:
> 400 + 1600 = 2000.

Finding the sizes of parts in this way is called **dividing in a given ratio**.

Example 7

Divide £50 in the ratio 2 : 3.

One share is $\frac{2}{5}$ of £50 and the other share is $\frac{3}{5}$ of £50.

$\frac{1}{5}$ of £50 = £50 ÷ 5 = £10.

So one share is 2 × £10 = £20 and the other share
is 3 × £10 = £30.

Check: £20 + £30 = £50.

This means you have to find sums of money
that add up £50 and that are in the ratio 2 : 3.

£ + £ = £50

You do this by finding each share as a
fraction of the total.
Add the two numbers in the ratio to get the
denominator.

More than two quantities can be divided in a given ratio.

Example 8

A company gives a bonus of £30 000 to a team of three employees,
Dave, James and Nicola.
The bonus is divided in the ratio of their earnings.
Dave earns £25 000, James earns £20 000 and Nicola earns £30 000.
Work out the bonus that each of them gets.

The ratio of Dave's to James' to Nicola's earnings

= £25 000 : £20 000 : £30 000

= 25 000 : 20 000 : 30 000

= 25 : 20 : 30 = 5 : 4 : 6

Dave gets $\frac{5}{15}$, James gets $\frac{4}{15}$ and Nicola gets $\frac{6}{15}$.

$\frac{1}{15}$ of £30 000 = £2000

So Dave gets 5 × £2000 = £10 000, James gets 4 × £2000 = £8000
and Nicola gets 6 × £2000 = £12 000.

Add the numbers in
the ratio to get the
denominator of the
fraction:
5 + 4 + 6 = 15

Check:
10 000 + 8000 + 12 000
= 30 000.

Exam practice 10C

1 a Divide 70p into two parts in the ratio 3 : 2.
   b Divide 64 m into two parts in the ratio 3 : 5.
   c Divide £54 into two shares in the ratio 4 : 5.
   d Divide £20 into two parts in the ratio 3 : 5.

2 Dave and Tim share 40 marbles between them in the ratio 3 : 5.
   How many do they each get?

3 Molly is 12 years old and Deborah is 18 years old.
   Divide £75 between them in the ratio of their ages.

First find the ratio of
their ages and simplify
it.

4 There are 30 pupils in a class.
   The ratio of the number of boys to the number of girls is 8 : 7.
   How many boys are there?

5 The area of a garden is 204 m².
   The ratio of the paved area to the unpaved area is 12 : 5.
   Find the unpaved area.

6 The fibres used to make shirt material are cotton and polyester in
   the ratio 3 : 2.
   How much polyester is there in a shirt that weighs 115 g?

7 Divide 6 m of string into three lengths in the ratio 3 : 7 : 2.

8 Divide £260 among three people so that their shares are in the
   ratio 4 : 5 : 4.

9 A 50 litre bag of compost is made by mixing sand, peat and
   fertilizer in the ratio 4 : 5 : 1.
   What volume of each ingredient is used?

10 The instructions for mixing paint to give a shade of green are:

   | Use colours 17, 139, 250 in the ratio 2 : 1 : 8. |

   Work out the quantity of colour 250 needed to give 10 litres of
   this shade of green.

11 The fuel tank on a moped holds 20 litres.
   The fuel must be a mixture of oil and petrol in the ratio 1 : 50.
   Work out how much oil is needed for a full tank.

12 Concentrated orange juice has to be diluted with water in the
   ratio 2 : 5 by volume.
   Find how many millilitres of concentrated juice are needed to
   make up 2 litres of juice to drink.

13 The tank on a chemical spray holds 5 litres.
   The instructions on a bottle of moss killer recommend dilution
   in the ratio 3 : 50.
   a How much moss killer should be put in to make a full tank of
      spray?
   b Work out the quantity of moss killer needed to make 3 litres
      of spray.

14 Bronze contains copper and tin in the ratio 2 : 11 by weight.
   Find the weight of copper needed to make 15 kg of this bronze.

15 Mr Peters, Mrs Jones and Mr Patel earn salaries of £15 000,
   £20 000 and £30 000 respectively.
   A bonus of £8000 is to be divided between these three employees
   in the ratio of their salaries.
   a Work out the ratio of their salaries.
   b What is the bonus that is paid to each employee?

Look at the quantities
given in the questions
to help you decide
how accurate your
answers should be.
When measurements
are given to 2 or 3
significant figures,
your answers need to
be correct to 2 or 3
significant figures.

16 Two students paid £176.40 for a new washing machine. They shared the cost in the ratio of the number of times they had each used the old machine.

  a Tom used the machine twice a week and Jane used it four times a week.
     How much should they each pay?

  b After they had paid the bill, Jane remembered that she had used the machine one more time each week to do a friend's wash.
     How much should she pay Tom?

10.4 Direct proportion

When two varying quantities are always in the same ratio they are **directly proportional**.
The instructions on a bottle of fertilizer are to dilute 5 ml of fertilizer with 500 ml of water.
You can vary the amounts of fertilizer and water but they must stay in the ratio 5 : 500. The amount of fertiliser is directly proportional to the amount of water.

> When two quantities are directly proportional, they behave in the same way.
> If one quantity is doubled, so is the other.
> If one quantity is quadrupled, so is the other.
> If one quantity is halved, so is the other.

Example 9

The mass of a lump of lead is directly proportional to its volume.
6 cm^3 of lead has a mass of 67.8 g.
Find the mass of 0.8 cm^3 of lead.

1 cm³ weighs $\frac{67.8}{6}$ g.

So 0.8 cm³ of lead has a mass of $\frac{67.8}{6} \times 0.8$ g = 9.04 g.

> First find the mass of 1 cm³.
> Then the mass of 0.8 cm³ is 0.8 times the mass of 1 cm³.

Exam practice 10D

  1 a The cost of 1 kg of sugar is 90p.
        What is the cost of 12 kg of sugar?

     b In one hour an electric fire uses $1\frac{1}{2}$ units.
        Find how many units it uses in $\frac{1}{2}$ hour.

     c The cost of 1 kg of mushrooms is £3.30.
        Find the cost of 2.4 kg of mushrooms.

> You can assume that the quantities in this exercise are directly proportional.

2   It costs 4.8p to run a fridge for 3.2 hours.
    a   Work out the cost of running the fridge for one hour.
    b   How long will the fridge run for on 1p?

3   A dog walked 16 km in 4 hours.
    Find how long it took him to cover 12 km.

4   An electric heater uses $12\frac{1}{2}$ units in 5 hours.
    a   How many units does it use in 3 hours?
    b   How long does the same heater take to use 20 units?

5   A hire car journey of 300 miles costs £84.
    At the same rate per mile find the cost of travelling 250 miles.

6   It costs £419 to turf a lawn of area 32 m².
    Work out how much it costs to turf a lawn of area 50 m².

7   A machine fills 750 cans in 6 hours.
    How many cans does it fill in 4 hours?

8   A 2 kg bag of sugar contains 9×10^6 crystals.
    How many crystals are there in 1.8 kg of this sugar?

9   The current flowing through a lamp is proportional to the
    voltage across the lamp.
    The current is 0.6 amps when the voltage across the lamp is
    10 volts.
    Work out the voltage needed to make a current of 0.9 amps flow.

10 Ten grains of rice weigh 1.5×10^{-3} kg.
    What is the weight of 1000 grains of rice?

11 The air resistance of a moving car is proportional to the speed at
    which the car is travelling.
    When a car is moving at 50 km/h, the air resistance is
    2500 newtons.
    What is the speed of this car when the air resistance is
    3500 newtons?

12 The instructions for making a model list the following materials:

Quantity	Costs
300 cm tape	1 m costs 76p
75 nails	250 nails cost £1.25
20 ml glue	100 ml costs £2.50
150 cm wood beading	2 m costs £1.08
2 sheets A4 card	a pack of 5 sheets costs £3.25

    Find the cost of making this model as accurately as possible,
    then give your answer correct to the nearest penny.

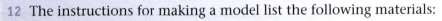

10.5 Inverse proportion

Two quantities are **inversely proportional** when their product is constant.

Inverse proportion is also called **indirect proportion**.

A car travels 10 miles.
If the car travels at 20 mph, it takes $\frac{1}{2}$ hour.
If the car travels at 40 mph, it takes $\frac{1}{4}$ hour.
The speed and time taken are inversely proportional because speed $\times$ time $= 10$.

> When two quantities are inversely proportional:
> If one quantity is doubled, the other is halved.
> If one quantity is quadrupled, the other is quartered.
> If one quantity is halved, the other is doubled.

Example 10

A tank is filled in 2 hours using 9 hoses.
How long does it take to fill the tank with 6 hoses?

$2 \times 9 = 18$
time $\times 6 = 18$,
time $= 18 \div 6 = 3$ hours.

> The time taken and the number of hoses are inversely proportional so their product is constant.

Exam practice 10E

1 A stack of hay will feed 20 cows for 9 days.
   How many days will the stack of hay last for 15 cows?

2 A batch of bottles can be packed in 30 boxes, each holding 12 bottles.
   How many boxes holding 9 bottles are needed to pack this batch?

3 A factory can make an order in 36 days using 40 production lines.
   How many days can the same order be made in using 45 production lines?

4 A pack of paper can be shared between 16 people, giving 5 sheets each.
   How many sheets would each person get if the same pack is shared between 20 people?

5 28 employees share a bonus, each getting £300.
   How much would each get if the same bonus is shared between 21 employees?

> **Class discussion**
> Which of these questions involve quantities that are directly proportional, inversely proportional or neither?
> - Using the exchange rate £2 = €3, how many euros are equal to £7?
> - A ten-year-old girl is 1.3 m tall. How tall will the girl be when she is 18?
> - A train travelling at an average speed of 80 mph takes 90 minutes for a journey. How long will the train take to cover the same distance travelling at an average speed of 100 mph?
> - Four towels take 3 hours to dry on a clothes line. How long will it take six towels to dry?

10.6 Writing equations for direct proportion

Writing an equation can help you to solve more complicated proportion questions.

The instructions on this petrol can show that the amount of oil and petrol are directly proportional. Although you can vary the amount of oil and petrol, the relationship between them is always the same; for every 1 unit of oil you need 50 units of petrol.

This relationship can be expressed as an equation. If x is the amount of oil, and y is the amount of petrol, then $y = 50x$.

Any two quantities that are directly proportional are related by an equation of the form $y = kx$ where k is a constant.

The symbol '$\propto$' means 'is proportional to', so $y \propto x$ means $y = kx$.

Example 11

The mass, m kg, of a square carpet tile is directly proportional to the square of the length, a cm, of its side. A tile of side 30 cm weighs 1200 g.

a Find the equation connecting m and a.

b Find the weight of a carpet tile of side 36 cm.

a $m = ka^2$

$1200 = k \times 30^2$ so $k = \dfrac{1200}{30^2} = \dfrac{1200}{900} = \dfrac{4}{3}$.

Therefore $m = \dfrac{4}{3}a^2$.

> m is directly proportional to the square of a, so m is directly proportional to a^2. They are related by the equation $m = ka^2$.
> You know that when $a = 30$, $m = 1200$ so you can substitute these values into the equation to find k.

b When $a = 36$, $m = \dfrac{4}{3} \times 36^2 = 1728$.

> You can use the equation connecting a and m to find m when $a = 36$.

A tile of side 36 cm weighs 1728 g.

10.7 Writing equations for inverse proportion

When two quantities are inversely proportional their product is constant.

Any two quantities that are inversely proportional are related by an equation of the form $xy = k$ where k is a constant.

> You can also write this equation as $y = \dfrac{k}{x}$.

When y is inversely proportional to x, $y \propto \dfrac{1}{x}$, so $y = \dfrac{k}{x}$.

Example 12

The time, t minutes, it takes a lorry to travel between junctions 6 and 7 on a motorway is inversely proportional to its speed, v mph.
The lorry takes 20 minutes when travelling at 55 mph.

a Find the equation connecting t and v.

b How long does it take the lorry when its speed is 60 mph?

a $tv = k$

$20 \times 55 = k$ so $k = 1100$

Therefore $tv = 1100$.

> As t and v are inversely proportional, they are related by the equation $tv = k$.
> Use $t = 20$ and $v = 55$ to find the value of k.

b When $v = 60$, $t \times 60 = 1100$,

so $\qquad t = \dfrac{1100}{60} = 18.3\ldots$

It takes the lorry 18 minutes to the nearest minute.

> Use $tv = 1100$ to find t when $v = 60$.

You do not need to know what the units are. As long as you know two quantities are directly proportional or inversely proportional, you can solve the problem.

Example 13

A quantity y is inversely proportional to the quantity $(x + 3)$.
When $x = 2$, $y = 10$.
Find the value of y when $x = 7$.

$y \propto \dfrac{1}{x+3}$

So $y(x + 3) = k$

$10(2 + 3) = k$ so $k = 50$

Therefore $y(x + 3) = 50$.

> First find the equation connecting x and y. As y and $x + 3$ are inversely proportional, their product is constant.
> Use $x = 2$ and $y = 10$ to find the value of the constant.

When $x = 7$, $y(7 + 3) = 50$

$\qquad\qquad 10y = 50$

So $\qquad\qquad y = 5$.

> Now you can substitute 7 for x in the equation and solve it to find y.

Exam practice 10F

1 y is directly proportional to the square of a quantity x.
When $x = 5$, $y = 100$.
Find the equation connecting x and y.

> The equation will be in the form $y = kx^2$.

2 V is inversely proportional to the square of a quantity l.
When $l = 1.5$, $V = 50$.
Find the equation connecting l and V.

> The equation will be in the form $Vl^2 = k$.

3 R is directly proportional to $\sqrt{A}$. When $A = 36$, $R = 3.4$.
Find the equation connecting A and R.

4 A quantity t is directly proportional to a quantity $(s^2 + 1)$.
   When $s = 3$, $t = 5$.
   a   Find the equation connecting s and t.
   b   Find the value of i t when $s = 1.2$ ii s when $t = 25$.

5 A quantity y is inversely proportional to $\sqrt{x}$.
   When $x = 144$, $y = 3$.
   a   Find the equation connecting x and y.
   b   Find the value of i x when $y = 5$ ii y when $x = 49$.

6 The number, n, of 4 mm thick square tiles that can be made from
   one batch of liquid plastic is inversely proportional to the square
   of the length, x cm, of a side of a square.
   When $n = 20$, $x = 15$
   a   Find the equation connecting n and x.
   b   How many squares of side 10 cm can be made from one batch
       of liquid plastic?

> n is inversely proportional to x^2 so the equation will be in the form $nx^2 = k$.

7 The volume, V cm^3, of smoothie in a bottle is directly
   proportional to the cube of the height, h cm, of the bottle.
   150 ml fills a bottle 15 cm high.
   a   Find the equation connecting V and h.
   b   How much smoothie will fill a bottle 30 cm high?

8 A quantity p is directly proportional to the cube of a quantity q.
   When $q = 2$, $p = 16$. Find
   a p when $q = 6$
   b q when $p = 250$.

9 A quantity T is inversely proportional to $(v - 4)$.
   If $T = 3$ when $v = 6$, find T when $v = 10$.

10 The maximum speed, v mph, that a bicycle can round a bend
    of radius r m without toppling over is directly proportional
    to $\sqrt{r}$.
    The maximum speed round a bend of radius 40 m is 25 mph.
    Find the maximum speed round a bend of radius 20 m.

11 A company scheme entitles employees to a pension that is
    directly proportional to the square root of the number of years
    they have worked for the company.
    Roger Smith received a pension of £16 500 p.a. after working for
    the company for 25 years.
    Anne Brown will retire next year after working for 30 years for
    the company. What will her pension be?

12 The consumption of diesel by a locomotive is directly
    proportional to the square of its speed.
    When the speed is 80 km/h it uses 60 litres of diesel each hour.
    How much diesel does it use when its speed is 160 km/h?

10.8 Graphs representing direct and inverse proportion

You can draw a graph to represent the equation connecting two directly or inversely proportional quantities.

When two varying quantities x and y are directly proportional, the equation connecting them is of the form $y = kx$. Any equation of this form gives a straight line passing through the **origin**.

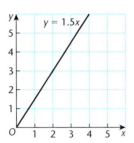

> This is true of any two quantities that are directly proportional. If p is directly proportional to q^2, then provided that values of p are plotted against values of q^2 you will get a straight line through the origin.

When two varying quantities x and y are inversely proportional, the equation connecting them is of the form $yx = k$ or $y = \frac{k}{x}$. The graph representing this equation looks like this.

> This is true of any two quantities that are inversely proportional. If p is inversely proportional to $(q + 1)$ then provided that values of p are plotted against values of $q + 1$ you will get a curve like the one shown here.

Exam practice 10G

1   A quantity x is directly proportional to a quantity y.
    Which of these graphs could represent the equation connecting x and y?

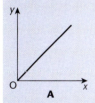
A

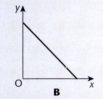
B

C

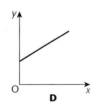
D

2   A quantity T is inversely proportional to a quantity s.
    a   Which of these graphs could represent the equation connecting T and s?
    b   Which graph could represent the relationship if the horizontal axis was labelled $\frac{1}{s}$ instead of s?

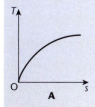
A

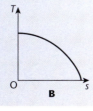
B

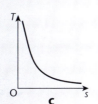
C

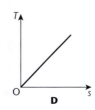
D

3 The cost, £*p*, of any article bought in Spain is directly
   proportional to its cost in euros, €*n*.
   a Find the equation connecting *p* and *n* when the exchange rate
      is £1 = €1.50.
   b Draw a graph to show the equation for values of *n* from 0 to
      100.

4 The time, *t* seconds, that an arrow takes to cover a fixed distance
   is inversely proportional to its speed, *v* m/s.
   The arrow takes 2 seconds at 20 m/s.
   a Find the equation relating *v* and *t*.
   b Copy and complete this table for values of *v* and *t*.

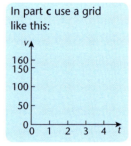

In part **c** use a grid
like this:

t	0.25	0.5	1	2	4
v	160		40		

   c Use these values to draw a graph showing the equation
      connecting *v* and *t*.

Summary of key points

- Ratios can be simplified by dividing the parts by the same number.
- Units can be left out of a ratio as long as they are the same.
- Ratios are related to fractions. If two quantities are in the ratio 2 : 3, then the first quantity is $\frac{2}{3}$ of the second quantity and the first quantity is $\frac{2}{2+3} = \frac{2}{5}$ of the total amount.
- You can divide a quantity in the ratio 2 : 3 by finding $\frac{2}{5}$ of the quantity and $\frac{3}{5}$ of the quantity.
- Two quantities are directly proportional when they are in a constant ratio to each other. This means that if one quantity is multiplied by a number, the other quantity is multiplied by the same number.
- Two quantities are inversely proportional when their product is constant. This means that if one quantity is doubled, the other is halved, and so on.
- The equation connecting two directly proportional quantities has the form $y = kx$ where k is a constant.
- The equation connecting two inversely proportional quantities has the form $yx = k$ or $y = \frac{k}{x}$ where k is a constant.

Most candidates who get GRADE C or above can:
- divide a quantity in a given ratio.

Most candidates who get GRADE A or above can also:
- find the equation relating quantities that are directly or inversely proportional.

Glossary

Direct proportion	two varying quantities that are always in the same ratio
Division in a given ratio	dividing a quantity so that the parts are in a given ratio
Indirect proportion	two varying quantities whose product is constant
Inverse proportion	the same as indirect proportion
Ratio	a comparison between the sizes of quantities
Origin	the point where the axes cross
The symbol:	used in ratios to mean 'to' so 2 : 3 means '2 to 3'

Examination practice paper

1 Use your calculator to work out

$$\frac{6.2 \times 2.8}{5.4 + 1.9}$$

  (a) Write down all the digits from your calculator display.   *(1 mark)*

  (b) Write your answer to 2 decimal places.   *(1 mark)*

2 To make 500 millilitres of squash you mix 80 ml of juice with 420 ml of water.

  (a) How much water is needed if 120 ml of juice is used?   *(2 marks)*

  (b) How much squash is made if 105 ml of water is used?   *(2 marks)*

3 (a) A shop has a CD priced at £10.20 before a sale.
In a sale the price is decreased by 15%.

    Work out the price of the CD in the sale.   *(3 marks)*

  (b) The number of these CDs sold by the shop increases from 150 per week
to 195 per week during the sale.

    Work out the percentage increase in the number of CDs sold per week.   *(3 marks)*

4 (a) Write 48 as the product of its prime factors.   *(2 marks)*

  (b) Find the highest common factor of 48 and 60.   *(2 marks)*

  (c) Find the least common multiple of 3, 4 and 5.   *(2 marks)*

5 Jenny reads in a magazine that the population of France is 5.9×10^7.
She says that this is less than 50 million.
Explain clearly why Jenny is not correct.   *(2 marks)*

6

> **Boxes of chocolates**
>
> $\frac{1}{3}$ **off the**
> **normal price**
>
> **Sale price £3.12**

Work out the normal price.   *(3 marks)*

7 The volume, V cubic metres, of a crate is directly proportional to its height, h metres.

A crate of height 2 metres has a volume of 40 cubic metres.

(a) Find an equation connecting V and h.   *(3 marks)*

(b) Work out the volume of a crate that has a height of 1.4 metres.   *(2 marks)*

8 A box contains 2200 grams of cereal. This amount is correct to 2 significant figures.

The cereal is to be poured into bowls which can each hold 40 grams. This amount is correct to the nearest 5 grams.

Work out the minimum number of bowls that can be filled with cereal.   *(4 marks)*

Section B

Time allowed: 40 minutes   Calculators are not allowed

1 A car travels 9 miles in a time of 15 minutes.

Calculate the average speed of the car.

Give your answer in miles per hour.   *(2 marks)*

2 Mel buys milk in 1 pint bottles.

He drinks $\frac{2}{3}$ of a pint of milk a day.

What is the least number of pints that he needs to buy for one week?   *(3 marks)*

3 Given that $365 \times 23.5 = 8577.5$,

work out

(a) 3650×235 *(1 mark)*

(b) $8577.5 \div 3.65$ *(1 mark)*

4 To make Gorgeous Green paint, blue and yellow paint are mixed together
in the following ratio.
$$\text{blue : yellow} = 5 : 2$$

How many litres of blue paint will be needed to make 56 litres of
Gorgeous Green paint?   *(2 marks)*

5 Work out

(a) $\frac{2}{5} - \frac{1}{4}$ *(2 marks)*

(b) the reciprocal of 0.2   *(2 marks)*

(c) $\dfrac{3^4 \times 3^8}{(3^2)^3}$

Give your answer as a power of 3.   *(3 marks)*

(d) $49^{-0.5}$ *(2 marks)*

6 In 2004 there were 400 members of a health club.
The number of members has increased by 10% each year since 2004.
Work out the number of members in 2006.   *(2 marks)*

7 Work out $4.83 \times 10^{-1} + 7 \times 10^{-2}$.   *(3 marks)*

8 The graph of $y = x^2 - 2x - 8$ is drawn for values of x between -3 and $+5$.

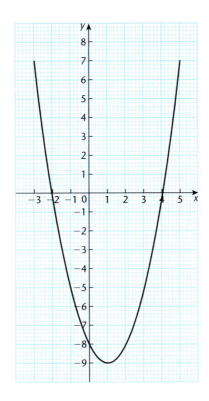

(a) Write down the negative solution of the equation $x^2 - 2x - 8 = 0$.   *(1 mark)*

(b) By drawing an appropriate linear graph, find the solutions of the equation

$$x^2 - 3x - 7 = 0$$ *(3 marks)*

9 (a) Show that $\sqrt{27} + \sqrt{12} - \sqrt{3} = 4\sqrt{3}$.   *(3 marks)*

(b) Write $(\sqrt{27} + \sqrt{12} - \sqrt{3})^{-2}$ as a fraction in its simplest form.   *(2 marks)*

Answers

Exam practice 1A

1 a 4 − 6 does not give 2.
   b Yes, 199 + 77 = 276.
   c yes
   d yes
2 843
3 3280
4 a 73   b 20   c 129
5 343
6 a 133   b 91   c 138   d 294   e 165
   f 243   g 217   h 97   i 56
7 4957
8 4033 m
9 159
10 154

Exam practice 1B

1 a 304   b 1989   c 1632
   d 924   e 2859   f 844
2 a 17   b 38   c 51
   d 27   e 37   f 123
3 1029, 7203
4 a 4   b 6   c 4
5 a 360   b 5100   c 108 000
   d 56 000   e 1380   f 14 400
   g 306 800   h 466 000   i 4 260 000

Exam practice 1C

1 a 60   b 330   c 20   d 150
2 a C   b B   c C   d B
3 Answer must be less than 737.
4 a 856 + 248 is bigger than 856.
   b Answer is bigger than 674.
   c 487 + 145 − 223 is about 487 − 80 which is less than 576.
   d 831 minus more than 800 is less than 100.
5 Too little, 6 × 29 is bigger than 50
6 a A and C   b A and B   c B and C
7 a A   b C
8 Should be 50 × 4 is 200, then multiply by 100 by moving the figures 2 places to the left, i.e. gives 20 000.

Exam practice 1D

1 a 26 000, 25 026   b 7200, 7098
   c 9000, 8750   d 45 000, 43 076
   e 25 000, 30 012
2 56 296 g
3 1428

4 2304
5 16
6 1152
7 a 1   b 1   c 5   d 4   e 7   f 3

Exam practice 1E

1 a 7   b 8   c 1   d 10
2 122
3 a 5   b 25
4 12
5 a 6   b Yes, 5.
6 34

Exam practice 1F

1 a 18   b 9   c 9   d 0   e 55   f 14
2 a 4   b 12   c 17   d 7   e 29   f 125
3 46
4 £3.65
5 560 cm
6 9
7 1872 or 1873 depending on whether or not he'd had his birthday.
8 a 1889 or 1890   b 115 or 116 years
9 55

Exam practice 1G

1 a −4, −2, 1   b −5, −4, −2
   c −3, −2, 3, 7   d −5, −3, 3, 5
2 a −9, −5, −3, −1, 0, 1
   b 6, 4, 0, −2, −4, −6
3 a −3   b 4   c −2   d 3   e −2
   f 13   g 4   h −4   i −20
4 a −2   b 6   c −2   d −10
   e 2   f −2
5 a 2   b −3   c 4   d −5   e 3
   f −6   g 2   h 2   i 2
6 83 °C
7 a 1 a.m.   b 3 p.m.
8 9 a.m.
9 23°
10 a i 8 p.m.   ii noon
    b 4 a.m. next day.

Exam practice 1H

1 a −8   b 7   c −26   d 10   e −6
   f 1   g 2   h 1   i 1   j 12
   k −1   l 7   m 20   n 4   p −23
2 +5 and −5
3 a −7   b −4   c 4   d 3

4 Multiply by -3.

5 a -2 b $128, -256$

6 a $4 = 1-(-3)$ b $2 + 3 = 5$
   c $6 = (-2) \times (-3)$ d $5 - (-2) = 7$
   e $2 + (-4) = -2$ f $5 - (-4) = 9$

7 a 20 b -10 c 10

8 £3800

9 £206

10 a 7 b -2

11 a -4 b -7 c 4

12 a -9 b 11 c 17

Exam practice 2A

1 a $1 \times 18, 2 \times 9, 3 \times 6$
   b $1 \times 36, 2 \times 18, 3 \times 12, 4 \times 9, 6 \times 6$
   c $1 \times 48, 2 \times 24, 3 \times 16, 4 \times 12, 6 \times 8$
   d $1 \times 60, 2 \times 30, 3 \times 20, 4 \times 15, 5 \times 12, 6 \times 10$
   e $1 \times 45, 3 \times 15, 5 \times 9$
   f $1 \times 144, 2 \times 72, 3 \times 48, 4 \times 36, 6 \times 24, 8 \times 18,$
     12×12

2 a Yes, $7 + 4 + 7 =18$ and $4 + 2 + 9 = 15$,
     both are divisible by 3.
   b No, $5+6+7+5 = 23$ which is not divisible
     by 3.

3 357, 88 551 and 33 447

4 368, 3897, 88 569, 33 444

5 29, 41, 101, 127

6 a $8 + 8 + 2 = 18$ which is divisible by 3 and
     8820 ends in 0 so is divisible by 5. Therefore
     8820 is divisble by 15.
   b No, 882 is not divisible by 8.

7 a Yes, even, so divides by 2, $2 + 1 + 1 + 6$
     $+ 8 = 18$ which is divisible by 3, so 21168 is
     divisible by 6.
   b Yes, $3+8+7 = 18$ which is divisible by 3;
     30 870 ends in 0 so is divisible by 5.
     Therefore 30 870 is divisible by 15.

8 a $8 = 3 + 5, 10 = 3 + 7, 12 = 5 + 7,$
     $14 = 3 + 11, 16 = 5 + 11, 18 = 5 + 13,$
     $20 = 3 + 17$ or $7 + 13$
   b $11 = 3 + 3 + 5, 13 = 3 + 5 + 5,$
     $15 = 5 + 5 + 5, 17 = 5 + 5 + 7,$
     $19 = 5 + 7 + 7, 21 = 7 + 7 + 7,$
     $23 = 5 + 7 + 11, 25 = 5 + 7 + 13,$
     $27 = 7 + 7 + 13, 29 = 3 + 7 + 19$

9 a No, 2 is a prime number.
   b No, 9 is odd but not prime.
   c true
   d true
   e No, 2,3,5,7 are the only primes less than 10.
   f $91 = 7 \times 13$ so is not a prime number.
     Largest prime less than 100 is 97.

10 Yes, $7 + 43, 13 + 37, 19 + 31$.

Exam practice 2B

1 a 2^3 b 3^3 c 7^4 d 5^5

2 a No, it is 3^6.
   b Yes, 6^4 means $6 \times 6 \times 6 \times 6$.

3 a 27 b 25 c 32 d 81

4 a No, $3^3 = 3 \times 3 \times 3 = 27$.
   b Yes, $2^4 = 2 \times 2 \times 2 \times 2 = 16$.

5 1, 4, 9, 16, 25, 36, 49, 64, 81, 100, 121, 144,
169, 196, 225

6 1, 8, 27, 64, 125, 216, 343, 512, 729, 1000,
1331, 1728, 2197, 2744, 3375

7 a $2^2 \times 5^2$ b $2^2 \times 3^3$ c $2^2 \times 3^2 \times 5^2$
   d $3^2 \times 5 \times 7^4$

8 No, $3^3 \times 5^2 \times 7^2$.

9 a 108 b 225 c 180 d 126

10 a 2^2 b 2^3 c 7^2 d 2^5 e 3^2 f 2^6
   g 5^4 h 7^5

Exam practice 2C

1 a 3 b 8 c 12 d 25 e 11 f 21

2 a 13 b 2 c 24 d 360

3 a No, 14 divides into both.
   b No, 8 will not divide into 36, 44 or 52.

4 a 5 b 18 c 4 d 36 e 18 f 9

5 50 cm

6 6 cm

7 21

8 7 cm

Exam practice 2D

1 a 6 b 30 c 72 d 60

2 a 36 b 48 c 24 d 360

3 a Yes, $15 = 3 \times 5, 18 = 2 \times 3^2$,
     so LCM $= 2 \times 3^2 \times 5 = 90$.
   b No, both go into 72.

4 1 minute (60 seconds)

5 45 cm

6 25th February, Thursday

7 2 minutes (120 sec)

8 840 sec

Exam practice 2E

1 a 4 or -4 b 5 or -5 c 9 or -9
   d 13 or -13 e 12 or -12

2 Yes, $(-16) \times (-16) = 256$.

3 20 and -20

4 a $484 = 2^2 \times 11^2, +22$
   b $324 = 2^2 \times 3^4, 18$ and -18

5 56

6 a 75 b 35 c 52
   d 196 e 60

7 a 5 b -2 c 10

8 No, $(3)^3 = 27$.

9 10

10 a $2^9, 8$ b $3^3 \times 5^3, 15$ c 12

11 -6

12 6

13 10

Exam practice 3A

1 a $\frac{4}{8}$ b $\frac{2}{8}$ c $\frac{6}{8}$

2 a $\frac{6}{12}$ b $\frac{8}{12}$ c $\frac{9}{12}$ d $\frac{2}{12}$

3 a $\frac{6}{45}$ b $\frac{20}{45}$ c $\frac{42}{45}$ d $\frac{27}{45}$

4 $\frac{2}{5} = \frac{4}{10} = \frac{6}{15} = \frac{10}{25}$
5 a $\frac{1}{12}$ b $\frac{3}{4}$ c $\frac{4}{7}$ d $\frac{3}{4}$
6 a $\frac{2}{5}$ b $\frac{2}{5}$ c $\frac{1}{2}$ d $\frac{3}{10}$

Exam practice 3B

1 a $2\frac{1}{4}$ b $5\frac{3}{10}$ c $5\frac{3}{8}$ d $6\frac{3}{11}$
2 a $\frac{5}{4}$ b $\frac{7}{3}$ c $\frac{13}{4}$ d $\frac{27}{4}$
3 a $4\frac{1}{8}$ b $4\frac{1}{2}$ c $4\frac{1}{5}$ d $1\frac{8}{9}$
4 $\frac{5}{7} = \frac{15}{21}$ and $\frac{2}{3} = \frac{14}{21}$ so $\frac{5}{7} > \frac{2}{3}$.
5 a $\frac{2}{9}$ b $\frac{2}{7}$ c $\frac{6}{7}$
6 a $\frac{1}{4}, \frac{2}{7}$ b $\frac{3}{5}, \frac{2}{3}, \frac{5}{6}$ c $\frac{1}{8}, \frac{2}{5}, \frac{7}{10}, \frac{19}{20}$
7 $\frac{5}{6}, \frac{7}{12}, \frac{1}{2}, \frac{1}{3}$
8 a $\frac{1}{3}, \frac{1}{4}, \frac{1}{5}, \frac{2}{5}$ b $\frac{1}{2}, \frac{2}{4}$ c $\frac{2}{3}, \frac{3}{5}, \frac{3}{4}, \frac{4}{5}$

Exam practice 3C

1 $\frac{1}{6}$
2 $\frac{3}{5}$
3 $\frac{3}{8}$
4 a $\frac{1}{4}$ b $\frac{13}{60}$ c $\frac{6}{125}$
5 $\frac{3}{8}$
6 a $\frac{1}{60}$ b $\frac{1}{6}$ c $\frac{3}{4}$ d $\frac{3}{5}$
7 a 90p b $\frac{7}{18}$
8 $\frac{3}{5}$
9 $\frac{7}{16}$
10 $\frac{5}{6}$
11 $\frac{2}{3}$
12 $\frac{37}{70}$

Exam practice 3D

1 a $\frac{13}{20}$ b $\frac{19}{20}$ c $\frac{1}{5}$ d $\frac{1}{6}$ e $\frac{8}{15}$ f $\frac{1}{6}$
2 a $\frac{53}{100}$ b $\frac{1}{2}$ c $3\frac{1}{20}$
3 a $4\frac{9}{20}$ b $4\frac{1}{4}$ c $1\frac{1}{10}$ d $1\frac{5}{6}$ e $\frac{7}{12}$ f $\frac{7}{12}$
4 a $\frac{3}{5}$ b 0 c $6\frac{7}{15}$
5 $\frac{23}{36}$
6 2.5 m
7 $\frac{1}{2}$ m
8 $1\frac{5}{8}$ feet

Exam practice 3E

1 a 33 miles b 21 litres c 28 km
   d 20 hours e 141p f 168 cm
   g 292 days h 35 min
2 a 2 days b £6 c 20 min
   d 40 sec e £1 f 27 cm
   g 3 cm h $22\frac{1}{2}$ ft i £21
   j 219 days k £34 l £84
3 a i 25 ii 24 b 11
4 a i 36 m ii 15 m b 9 m
5 a £840 b £280 c $\frac{1}{2}$
6 a 9 km b 6 km c 3 km

7 90
8 Donna £1876, Julian £1608, Maria £1876
9 a 686 b 1372 c 2401
10 80
11 1

Exam practice 3F

1 a $\frac{2}{15}$ b $\frac{6}{49}$ c $\frac{5}{24}$ d $\frac{14}{81}$ e $\frac{1}{6}$ f $\frac{4}{7}$
   g $\frac{1}{6}$ h $\frac{3}{4}$ i $\frac{2}{5}$ j $\frac{5}{48}$ k $\frac{7}{18}$ l $\frac{6}{7}$
2 a $\frac{2}{9}$ b $\frac{1}{7}$
3 a 1 b $1\frac{1}{8}$ c 5 d $\frac{1}{2}$ e $1\frac{2}{5}$ f 30
   g $4\frac{1}{2}$ h 20 i $13\frac{1}{2}$ j 50 k 32 l 36
4 a $\frac{9}{14}$ b $1\frac{3}{4}$ c $3\frac{1}{3}$
5 a $\frac{5}{3}$ b $\frac{9}{7}$ c $\frac{1}{4}$ d $\frac{1}{6}$
   e $\frac{2}{5}$ f $\frac{4}{13}$ g $\frac{4}{11}$
6 a $\frac{3}{4}$ b $\frac{2}{3}$ c 6 d 5 e $6\frac{2}{3}$ f $\frac{5}{6}$
   g $4\frac{5}{6}$ h 39 i $\frac{1}{40}$ j 1 k $\frac{1}{6}$ l 6
7 a $\frac{7}{10}$ b 6 c $\frac{3}{8}$ d $\frac{27}{28}$
8 a $\frac{1}{6}$ b $1\frac{2}{3}$
9 6
10 $1\frac{1}{4}$ m
11 a $1\frac{1}{2}$ m b 1 m
12 $\frac{5}{8}$ m $\times \frac{1}{2}$ m
13 16
14 56
15 $5\frac{1}{4}$ m
16 $8\frac{8}{9}$ min
17 $3\frac{1}{3}$
18 a 29 b $\frac{1}{16}$ m

Exam practice 4A

1 a 0.4 b 0.15 c 0.63 d 0.3
2 a 7 hundredths b 7 tens
   c 7 hundredths d 7 tenths
   e 7 units f 7 thousandths
3 a 3.59 b 25.64 c 5
4 a 6.71 b 85.37 c 6
5 a 14.09, 13.75, 12.6, 12.55
   b 7.555, 7.55, 7.5, 7.05
6 a $\frac{1}{5}$ b $\frac{1}{2}$ c $\frac{3}{50}$ d $\frac{7}{10}$ e $\frac{4}{5}$ f $\frac{1}{40}$
7 a 1.9 b 2.35 c 1.8 d 1.38
   e 1.94 f 5.67 g 0.46 h 0.7
8 a 1.3 b 0.32 c 1.13 d 4.77
   e 10.5 f 12 g 3.7 h 4.3
9 18.08 cm
10 2.34 cm
11 £27.80
12 9.5 cm
13 3638.8
14 18.78 mm
15 9.22 mm
16 60p
17 9.44 cm

Exam practice 4B

1. a 250 b 0.66 c 24 400
   d 10 e 90 f 32
   g 36 h 140
2. a 0.46 b 0.000 85 c 1.2
   d 0.096 e 0.03 f 0.12
   g 0.005 h 0.021
3. a 0.48 b 0.024 c 0.0088
   d 0.0021 e 0.12 f 0.01
   g 4.5 h 0.0001
4. a 3 b 10 c 20
   d 0.3 e 990 f 333.75
   g 7 h 0.9
5. a 3.072 b 30 c 0.135
   d 0.07 e 0.4 f 0.266
   g 3 h 4.41 i 240
   j 12 500 k 1.2 l 73.5
6. a 0.008 b 50 c 0.81
7. a £170.30 b £1.89
8. £2980.40
9. £2.14 (nearest p)
10. 19.68 mm
11. 25.1 cm
12. a 22.4 b 37
13. 0.09

Exam practice 4C

1. a 300 b 40 c 140
   d 0 e 400 f 0.69
   g 40.38 h 28.8
2. a 13.5 b 1.00 c 77.998
   d 2.253 e 1.0028 f 0.05077
3. a 0.2 b 0.125 c 0.75
   d 0.6 e 0.15 f 0.25
   g 0.875 h 0.24
4. a $\frac{2}{5}$ b $\frac{4}{5}$ c $\frac{7}{8}$
5. a 0.6 b 0.66 c 1.8
6. $\frac{5}{3} = 1.667$, $1\frac{2}{7} = 1.286$, $\frac{15}{11} = 1.364$;
   $1\frac{2}{7}$, $\frac{15}{11}$, 1.49, 1.57, $\frac{5}{3}$
7. $\frac{6}{25}$, $\frac{3}{16}$, $\frac{2}{13}$, 0.105, 0.05
8. $\frac{1}{3}$ is 0.$\dot{3}$ to 1 d.p., but this is not exact.

Exam practice 4D

1. a 0.$\dot{7}$ b 0.0$\dot{3}$ c 0$\dot{1}\dot{8}$ d 26.3$\dot{5}$
   e 0.02$\dot{5}$ f 0.7$\dot{1}\dot{8}$ g 6.0$\dot{2}0\dot{5}$ h 1.3$\dot{4}8\dot{9}$
2. a 6 b 19 c 53 d $\frac{94}{10}$
3. a 0.266667 b 2.1257576 c 0.031461
4. a 0.$\dot{3}$ b 0.$\dot{1}4285\dot{7}$
   c 0.0$\dot{7}692\dot{3}$ d 0.1$\dot{8}$
5. a $\frac{5}{6}$ b 0.8$\dot{3}$
6. a 0.$\dot{6}$ b 0.$\dot{2}8571\dot{4}$ c 0.1$\dot{6}$ d 0.2$\dot{6}$
   e 0.$\dot{2}$ f 0.08$\dot{3}$ g 0.$\dot{3}8461\dot{5}$
   h 0.0$\dot{9}$ i 0.2$\dot{7}$ j 0.$\dot{6}\dot{3}$
7. 0.316 316 316

8. 0.461 538 461 538
9. a 0.1$\dot{3}$ b 0.01$\dot{3}$ c 0.001$\dot{3}$
10. a $\frac{8}{9}$ b $\frac{7}{9}$ c $\frac{5}{90}$ or $\frac{1}{18}$ d $\frac{5}{11}$ e $\frac{7}{11}$ f $\frac{38}{990}$
    g $\frac{1}{300}$ h $\frac{8}{37}$ i $\frac{1}{55}$ j $\frac{28}{37}$ k $1\frac{4}{9}$ l $2\frac{13}{90}$

Exam practice 5A

1. a 4 b 9 c 2 d 8
   e 6 f 2 g 2 h 5
2. a 6 b 8 c 0 d 7 e 7 f 5
3. a 30 b 0.6 c 8000
   d 600 e 2 f 5
   g 0.08 h 50
4. a 40 b 469 c 0.057
   d 46.1 e 0.0560 f 88.81
   g 3.07 h 3.509
5. a 2700 b 37 000 c 68 000
   d 73 000 e 9900 f 590
   g 890 h 1000
6. a 64.9 b 0.0764 c 0.006 44
   d 355 e 4.87 f 0.376
   g 10.6 h 0.004 67
7. a 1.7 b 8.3 c 0.063 d 18
8. a 4 b 0.048 c 4000
   d 0.0006 e 7.05 f 5.58
9. a 50, smaller b 0.008, larger
   c 50, larger d 0.010, larger
10. a 52.6, rounded up
    b 0.0409, rounded down
    c 1.21, rounded up
    d 0.000 222, rounded up
11. a 3 b 3
12. No, this is rounded to 2 s.f.
13. No, this is to the nearest 10 cm.
14. a 0.233 b 0.0256
    c 0.000 186 d 1.56
15. 46 kg

Exam practice 5B

1. a 150 b 60 c 240 d 20
   e 36 f 4 g 12 000 h 450
   i 4050 j 0.06 k 0.12 l 3
2. a 25 b 0.0016 c 0.09
   d 0.75 e 270 f 0.14
   g 3 h 28 i 17
3. £3000
4. a too big b too small
   c too small d too small
   e too big f too big
5. a B b D c A d B
6. e.g. a 100 b 7 c 1.5 d 30
7. e.g. a 0.2 b 100 c 0.7
8. e.g. 0.16 cm²
9. e.g. a £1800
   b below, all numbers rounded down
10. e.g. a 54 000
    b 216 000, far too high
11. Answer must be bigger than 2.13
12. C

Exam practice 5C

All these answers are examples. Any reasonable answer is acceptable.

1 a 10 b 20 c 70 d 90 e 110
2 a 0.8 b 0.9 c 0.1 d 0.05
3 a 0.3 b 0.2 c 0.06 d 0.09
  e 0.01 f 0.007
4 a 5 b 10 c 0.3 d 80
5 a 5 b 4 c 100

Exam practice 5D

1 a 156 b 13.4 c 12.9 d 42.2
2 a 1050 b 12600 c 0.536 d 1530
  e 0.291 f 0.0460 g 189 h 1450
  i 5.29 j 0.546
3 a 0.0181 b 3.28 c 6.01 d 0.636
  e 11.5 f 1.05 g 0.217 h 0.252
4 a 1.80 b 2.82 c 23.3 d 0.845
5 a 3.46 b 7.35 c 11.0
6 a 2.71 b 4.64 c 0.585
7 a 3.71 (3 s.f.) b 1.71
  c Find 2×1.5 or 2.5×1.5.
8 29, nearest whole number
9 a Must be less than 250 since more than 1 g is used in each cup.
  b 208, rounded down
10 £38.34 (nearest p)
11 a and b $\frac{1}{1-1}$, because denominator is 0 and you cannot divide by 0.
  c $\frac{1.3}{1.2-1} = \frac{1.3}{0.2} = 6.5$ d 4.88 (3 s.f.)

Exam practice 6A

1 a 3^8 b 7^7 c 9^{10} d 2^9
  e 4^{16} f 5^8 g 12^9 h 6^9
2 No, $10^4 \times 10^3 = 10^7$. Add not multiply indices.
3 Yes, $10^9 \times 10^8 = 10^{17}$.
4 a 7^2 b 2^2 c $5^1 = 5$ d 3^3
  e 2^2 f $5^1 = 5$ g 3^3 h 5^8
5 No, $y^{10} \div y^6 = y^{10-6} = y^4$. Subtract not divide indices.
6 a 1 b 4 c a d x^5
  e m^4 f b^3 g 1 h p^{14}
7 a 2^{12} b 5^{10} c 0.3^9
8 a 1 b 4 c 1 d 16
  e 25 f a^8
9 No, $4^0 = 1$ so answer is $\frac{1}{2^4} = \frac{1}{16}$

Exam practice 6B

1 a $\frac{1}{8}$ b $\frac{1}{9}$ c $\frac{1}{16}$ d $\frac{1}{100}$ e $\frac{1}{3}$ f $\frac{1}{125}$
2 a $\frac{1}{1000}$ b $\frac{1}{100000}$ c $\frac{1}{10000}$ d $\frac{1}{10}$
3 a 0.0001 b 0.01 c 0.001 d 0.000001
4 a 3^2 b 4^{-1} c 2^{-7} d 4^3
  e 2^2 f 3^{-5} g 3^{-2} h 2^{-2}
  i 3^{-9} j 3^6 k 5^4 l 2^3
5 a $\frac{8}{9}$ b $\frac{8}{25}$ c $\frac{1}{2592}$ d $\frac{25}{4}$
  e $\frac{1}{72}$ f 2

6 a 5^{-2} b 2^{-4} c 10^{-2} d 7^{-3}
  e 5^{-5} f 10^{-12}
7 a 10^1 b 10^0 c 10^{-1} d 10^{-2}
  e 10^{-3} f 10^{-6}
8 a $\frac{1}{2}$ b $\frac{1}{16}$ c 5
9 a $\frac{1}{4}$ b $\frac{1}{625}$ c 16 d 9 e 5
  f 2 g $\frac{9}{4}$ h $\frac{1}{2}$ i $\frac{64}{81}$

Exam practice 6C

1 a 2 b 3 c 4 d 6 e 3 f 4
  g 5 h 6 i $\frac{1}{2}$ j $\frac{1}{9}$ k $\frac{1}{10}$ l $\frac{1}{3}$
2 a $\frac{1}{2}$ b $\frac{1}{6}$ c $\frac{2}{5}$ d $\frac{3}{8}$
  e 0.1 f 0.5 g 0.2 h 0.9
3 a $\frac{1}{2}$ b $\frac{2}{3}$ c $\frac{5}{4}$ d $\frac{3}{2}$
  e 2 f 5 g $\frac{2}{3}$ h 10
4 a 8 b 9 c 125 d 25
  e 0.04 f 0.216 g 100 h 27
5 a 16 b 1728 c 16 d 0.09
  e $\frac{4}{9}$ f $\frac{4}{25}$ g $\frac{1}{100}$ h $\frac{32}{3125}$

Exam practice 6D

1 a $2\sqrt{3}$ b $5\sqrt{2}$ c $2\sqrt{2}$ d $3\sqrt{7}$
  e $10\sqrt{2}$ f $4\sqrt{3}$ g $6\sqrt{2}$ h $2\sqrt{7}$
2 a $\sqrt{10}$ b 4 c 5 d $5\sqrt{2}$
  e 6 f 8 g 7 h 6
3 a $\frac{\sqrt{3}}{3}$ b $\frac{\sqrt{5}}{5}$ c $\sqrt{3}$ d $\sqrt{5}$
  e $\frac{\sqrt{10}}{5}$ f $\sqrt{7}$ g $\sqrt{14}$ h $\frac{\sqrt{6}}{3}$
  i $\frac{\sqrt{2}}{2}$ j $\frac{2\sqrt{3}}{3}$
4 a $\frac{\sqrt{2}}{3}$ b 1 c $\frac{\sqrt{2}}{2}$ d $\frac{1}{5}$ e 1
5 a $\sqrt{2} - 1$ b $\frac{2\sqrt{3} + 3}{3}$
  c $\sqrt{3} + 2$ d $\frac{3\sqrt{5} + 5}{5}$

Exam practice 6E

1 a 5500 b 316 000
  c 4 155 000 d 577.8
  e 13 000 f 9150
  g 80 220 h 200 400 000
  i 7 400 000 j 20 400 000
  k 7402 l 310 100 000 000
2 a 0.0047 b 0.000 013 5
  c 0.000 310 3 d 0.771
  e 0.000 029 f 0.000 801
  g 0.050 08 h 0.000 000 020 52
  i 0.000 51 j 0.0635
  k 0.000 006 027 l 0.000 000 000 388 9
3 a 3780 b 5 300 000
  c 0.000 000 064 3 d 0.000 477
  e 0.001 26 f 740 000 000 000 000
  g 4 250 000 000 000 h 0.000 000 908

4 a 2.8×10^3 b 4.2×10^2
   c 3.907×10^4 d 7.604×10^4
   e 4.5×10^6 f 5.47×10^5
   g 1.53×10^4 h 4.3×10^7
   i 2.6×10^5 j 4×10^4
   k 5.091×10^6 l 7.04×10^2

5 a 3.6×10^{-2} b 7.7×10^{-1}
   c 7.07×10^{-1} d 8.4×10^{-3}
   e 3.5×10^{-2} f 9.6×10^{-3}
   g 4.02×10^{-2} h 6.6×10^{-6}
   i 4.9×10^{-5} j 7×10^{-9}
   k 6.022×10^{-4} l 8×10^{-2}

6 a 6.84×10^{-1} b 7.3×10^{-11}
   c 1.1×10^{-3} d 5.35×10^{-2}
   e 8.892×10^1 f 5.06×10^{-5}
   g 5.7×10^{-8} h 5.03×10^8

7 5.976×10^{24} kg

8 1.9×10^{30} kg

9 1 000 000 000 000 decibels

10 1.5×10^8 km

11 0.000 0708 cm

12 a 5.76×10^8, 2×10^{10}, 9.97×10^8, 2.47×10^5,
    3.75×10^4;
    37500, 247 000, 576 000 000, 997 000 000,
    20 000 000 000
   b 5.27×10^{-3}, 6.0005×10^{-1}, 9.906×10^{-1},
    5.02×10^{-8}, 3.005×10^{-3};
    0.000 000 050 2, 0.003 005, 0.005 27, 0.600
    05, 0.9906
   c 7.05×10^{-2}, 7.08×10^0, 7.93×10^1,
    7.00809×10^{-3}, 5.608×10^5;
    0.007 008 09, 0.0705, 7.08, 79.3, 560 800

13 9

14 4.8×10^{10}

Exam practice 6F

1 a 6×10^8 b 8×10^{13}
   c 2.1×10^{11} d 1.6×10^{11}
   e 8.4×10^7 f 1.08×10^{10}
   g 8×10^{11} h 1.35×10^{14}

2 a 6×10^2 b 1.8×10^7
   c 3×10^{-2} d 6×10^2
   e 1.08×10^4 f 7.4×10^{-6}
   g 8×10^{-6} h 1.4×10^{-5}
   i 1.86×10^{-15} j 2.64×10^{-10}

3 a 4×10^3 b 5×10^4
   c 3.5×10^3 d 7.5×10^2
   e 2×10^{-3} f 3×10^{-5}
   g 4×10^{-9} h 5×10^{-11}
   i 4×10^6 j 9×10^{-2}
   k 1.2×10^7 l 5×10^3

4 a 1.5×10^2 b 5×10^6
   c 5×10^2 d 1×10^6
   e 5×10^{-5} f 3×10^{-2}

5 a 3.66×10^3 b 5×10^3
   c 5×10^{-3} d 4.6×10^5
   e 2.89×10^5 f 9×10^{-4}

6 a 3.8×10^{-3} b 3.7×10^{-2}
   c 7.5×10^0 d 1.6×10^{-7}

7 a 2×10^4 b 2.9×10^3
   c 2.56×10^{-1} d -3×10^0

Exam practice 6G

1 a 94 300   b 62 800   c 0.000 062 6
   d 0.000 033 1   e 13.8   f 0.000 003 53

2 a 548 176   b 30 613
   c 0.2564   d 0.71

3 1.7×10^{-3} sec

4 3 000 000 m (3 s.f.)

5 1.70×10^{-24} g

6 750 g

7 £1.7×10^7 g

8 a 6.74×10^9 km   b 5.16×10^9 km

9 1.84×10^{-2} g

10 31.7 years (3 s.f.)

Exam practice 7A

1 a 200   b 60

2 1.72 m

3 a 250 cm   b 69.3 cm
   c 1200 m   d 4.55 km
   e 1.536 m   f 250 m

4 0.57 m, 156 cm, 2889 mm, 3.8 m, 25 m

5 a 16 km   b 64 km
   c 50 miles   d 30 cm
   e 16 inches   f 0.96 ha

6 1500 mm, 100 cm, 24 inches, 1 foot

7 2.23 km

8 38 mm (nearest mm)

9 Yes, $84 \times 0.621 = 52.164$.

10 160 mm and plane it down.

11 $\frac{125}{381}$

12 $\frac{1}{8}$

13 No, $\frac{1}{2}$ mile = 880 yds.

14 No, it's too big, room is 3 m by 3.6 m.

15 £6.08 (nearest p)

16 61 m^3 (nearest whole number)

17 6 ha

Exam pactice 7B

1 a 2500 g   b 4.5 t

2 a 0.5 kg   b 1300 kg   c 0.25 t
   d 1350 g   e 45.5 t   f 0.012 t

3 0.06 t, 62 000 g, 655 kg

4 a 11 lb   b 1.1 lb   c 20 kg

5 11 lb, 2.5 kg, 64 oz, 1500 g

6 $\frac{1}{5}$

7 65.2 kg

8 No, 4 oz = 113.6 g which is greater than 100 g.

9 $\frac{1}{10}$

Exam practice 7C

1 a 1000 cl   b $\frac{3}{10}$

2 a 2000 ml   b 250 ml   c 0.5 litres

3 50 cl, 0.46 litres, 400 ml, 0.05 litres, 40 ml

4 8

5 1 litre, 1 gallon, 10 pints

6 Midway between the 2 and 2.5 gallon marks.

7 16

8 22.5 litres

9 264 nearest litre

10 Yes, capacity is $150 \times 150 \times 100$ cm^3
    = 2250 litres = $\frac{2250}{4.5}$ gal = 500 gal.

Exam practice 7D

1 a 68 °F   b 14 °F
2 a 27 °C
  b −12 °C, both nearest whole number
3 38 °C nearest whole number
4 a 113 °F
  b 158 °F
  c 136 °F, nearest whole numbers
5 a 121 °C
  b 38 °C
  c 28 °C, nearest whole numbers

Exam practice 7E

1 a 15 km/h   b 112.5 mph
  c 4 km/h   d 50 mph
  e 27 km/h   f 6 mph
  g $3\frac{3}{4}$ mph   h 40 mph
2 a 45 metres per sec
  b 162 km per hour
3 $11\frac{1}{9}$ metres per sec
4 5.2 miles per hour
5 4 hrs 20 min
6 25 sec
7 $1\frac{1}{2}$
8 a 109 km/h
  b 95 km/h, both to nearest whole number
9 1.34 sec (3 s.f.)
10 762 sec (3 s.f.)
11 113 km/h (3 s.f.)

Exam practice 7F

1 3200 g
2 980 g
3 2314 g
4 618 g (3 s.f.)
5 6800 g or 6.8 kg

Exam practice 7G

1 a €84.5   b 536 lira
  c $270
2 £316, nearest £
3 80 000 yen
4 a £192 (3 s.f.)   b £15.38
5 a €18   b £80
6 61.60 rupees
7 London
8 a £1 = €1.52   b £1 = €1.64
9 a US$127.50   b £21.05
10 Florida £151 compare £168 Spain, £160 London.

Exam practice 7H

1 $5.55 \le w < 5.65$ where weight of bag is w kg.
2 £2450
3 $1.245 \le d < 1.255$ where d is diameter in mm.
4 a Gap, g m, is such that $1.645 \le g < 1.655$.
  b 1651 mm = 1.651 m which is within the range.

5 The smallest possible inside measurement (34.15 mm) is smaller than the largest possible side length for the cube (34.5 mm)
6 95 m
7 10.125 kg i.e. $10\frac{1}{8}$ kg
8 a 10 200   b 9750
9 a to nearest g   b 7.75 g
10 39 cm
11 364 days or 365 if a leap year.
12 a 26.1 cm²   b 24.9 cm² both to 3 s.f.
13 No, 80 000 × 0.75 inches = 60 000 inches which is less than 1 mile.
14 12
15 7.71 km/h (3 s.f.)
16 $1.76 \le h < 1.79$ (3 s.f.)
17 4224 cm³ (4 s.f.)
18 126 kg (3 s.f.)
19 a 9.905 208 333   b 23.067 188 66
  c 0.816046966
20 1.62 (3 s.f.)

Exam practice 8A

1 a 0.14   b 1.3   c 0.175
  d 0.4575   e 0.006
2 a $\frac{1}{4}$ b $\frac{1}{8}$ c $1\frac{1}{10}$
3 a 54%   b 80%   c 105%   d 5%
4 a 62.5%   b 75%   c 150%
  d $16\frac{2}{3}$%   e $66\frac{2}{3}$%   f $133\frac{1}{3}$%
5 Missing values are: 35%, 035, $\frac{131}{200}$, 0.655, $\frac{557}{200}$, 278.5, $\frac{5}{4}$, 1.25.

Exam practice 8B

1 a 8.3%   b 55.6%   c 313.3% (all to 1 d.p.)
2 a $166\frac{2}{3}$% b $216\frac{2}{3}$%   c $58\frac{1}{3}$%
3 $41\frac{2}{3}$%
4 $33\frac{1}{3}$%
5 a $\frac{15}{52}$ b $28\frac{11}{13}$% or 28.8% (3 s.f.)
6 0.175
7 $\frac{1}{3} = 33\frac{1}{3}$% which is more than 33%.

Exam practice 8C

1 a £20   b 3p   c £1.30
  d £43   e £264   f £3.90
2 a £18   b £500   c £450
  d 50 m   e 225 litres   f £1875
3 £437.50
4 39p
5 £6250
6 £4.23 (nearest p)
7 £3200
8 a £199.20   b £2.49   c £235
  d £55.20   e £25.15   f 167 g
  g 3.51 cm   h 150   i 67 miles
  j 6.5 min
9 127.5 sq m
10 £15.73
11 £2160
12 a 12 346 000 (nearest 1000)
  b 5 056 000 (nearest 1000)

13 249
14 £55
15 It means 30% of each ticket which is the same as 30% of the combined cost.

Exam practice 8D

1 a 3.125%   b 45%
   c 1%   d 10%
2 a $58\frac{1}{3}$%   b $66\frac{2}{3}$%
   c $112\frac{1}{2}$%   d $133\frac{1}{3}$%
3 30%
4 26.0% 1 d.p.
5 25.2%
6 $3\frac{1}{2}$%
7 7.8% 1 d.p.
8 24%
9 109% (nearest whole number)

Exam practice 8E

1 a i 1.08   ii 1.35   iii 1.175
   b i 0.88   ii 0.85   iii 0.9575
2 72.8 kg
3 a £540.60   b £100
4 a 497   b 5%
5 a $12\frac{1}{2}$%   b 253
6 a £999, nearest £   b £8.40
7 a 31   b 5
8 £2376
9 $33\frac{1}{3}$
10 a profit of £175   b 14.6%
11 29% nearest whole number
12 9 miles per litre
13 a 89.6p   b 616 litres
    c i £8.06   ii 1.44% decrease
14 £33 972

Exam practice 8F

1 £11.74
2 £650
3 £260
4 865 cm³
5 71 cm
6 71p
7 £35545, nearest £
8 £161.84
9 a £69.99   b £10.50
10 a £217.39   b £32.61
11 £15.19
12 €2.59
13 £546.34
14 £19 565

Exam practice 8G

1 £258.83
2 a 10 200   b 8670
3 a i £8000 ii £6800   b £3200
4 95.22 kg
5 £2754
6 a and b He thought the second 10% was on the original cost whereas it was on the discounted cost i.e. 10% of £90.

7 a £59.82   b £56.70
8 a £652.31   b £1616.30   c £2173.77
9 £186 624
10 £76 (nearest £)
11 a £4.90   b £5.10
12 £41 310
13 a £4608   b 48.8%
14 109.35 cm
15 £34 661.81
16 £6100
17 a 13 868   b 16 873   c 5
18 4
19 5
20 985
21 4
22 4 hours
23 £24.32
24 Both the same. For Sally find
    $10\,000 \times 1.1 \times 1.1 \times 1.1 \times 0.7$
    and for George find
    $10\,000 \times 0.7 \times 1.1 \times 1.1 \times 1.1$

Exam practice 9A

1 a $15a^2$ b $15p^2$ c $8xy$ d $30b$
   e $12x$ f $6s^2t$ g $6a^3b$ h $6a$
   i $-10t^2$ j $15st$ k $8ab$ l $24xy$
2 a $4x$ b $2x$ c $4x$
   d $6-a$ e $8x+5$ f $5x+y$
   g $12p-6$ h $-3a-6b$ i $-5x+4$
3 a x^2+8x b a^2+3a+3
   c $2a^2-2a+9$ d $x^2+2xy-2$
   e $5p^2+2p+6$ f $-y^2+y+7$
   g $7x^2-10x+4$ h $a^2-11a+8$
   i $4t^2-8t+8$
4 a $5\sqrt{3}$ b $4\sqrt{2}$ c $3\sqrt{3}$ d $7\sqrt{2}$
   e $4\sqrt{3}$ f 0 g $2\sqrt{2}$ h $3\sqrt{3}$

Exam practice 9B

1 a $10-6x$ b $28y-12y^2$
   c $6p^2q-4pq^2$ d $2a^2-8a+9$
   e $3x^2-7x-8$ f $6x-6y$
   g $x^2+xy+6y^2$ h $5x-13y$
   i $-x^2+5x-4$
2 a $2x^2-7x-4$ b $-10a^2+41a-21$
   c $10x^2+23x+12$ d $6s^2+st-2t^2$
   e $14y^2+69y+27$ f $4t^2-13t+3$
   g x^2-4 h $9x^2-1$
   i $2y^2-9y+10$ j x^2+6x+9
   k $x^2-10x+25$ l $4x^2+4x+1$
   m $9x^2-6x+1$ n $4x^2+12x+9$
   p $16-24x+9x^2$
3 a $\sqrt{2}-2$ b $3+2\sqrt{2}$ c -1
   d $3-2\sqrt{2}$ e $10-3\sqrt{5}$ f $20\sqrt{3}-15$
   g $\sqrt{6}-3$ h $13-4\sqrt{3}$ i -75
4 $3\sqrt{2}(\sqrt{18}-\sqrt{8}) = 3 \times \sqrt{36} - 3\sqrt{16}$
   $= 3 \times 6 - 3 \times 4 = 6$
5 $6-2\sqrt{2}+3\sqrt{3}-\sqrt{6}$

6   $-25 - 5\sqrt{3}$

7   $(\sqrt{18} + \sqrt{8})(\sqrt{18} - \sqrt{8}) = 18 - 8 = 10$

8   $a = -10,\ b = 2$

Exam practice 9C

1   If $x = 0.3$, $x^2 = 0.09$ so $x^2 < x$.

2   If x, $x + 1$ and $x + 2$ are integers their sum is $3x + 3$ which is divisible by 3.

3   $2 + 3 = 5$ which is odd.

4   If n is any integer, $2n + 1$ is odd. $(2n + 1)^2$ $= 4n^2 + 4n + 1$ which is odd because it does not divide exactly by 2.

5   Any even number $= 2n$ where n is a whole number, then $(2n)^2 = 4n^2$ which is divisible by 4.

6   For any two numbers, m and n, $(2m + 1)(2n + 1)$ is the product of two odd numbers and equals $4mn + 2m + 2n + 1$ which is odd because it does not divide exactly by 2.

Exam practice 9D

1   Missing values are 10 and -8.

2   a

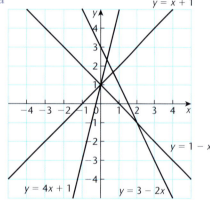

   b $(\frac{2}{3}, 1\frac{2}{3})$

3   a $y = 2x + 3$ b $y = \frac{5}{4}x + 3$

   c $y = -\frac{7}{5}x - 2$ d $y = -2x + \frac{2}{3}$

   e $y = x - 2$ f $y = \frac{2}{3}x - \frac{2}{3}$

4   a   b $(-\frac{1}{2}, \frac{5}{2})$

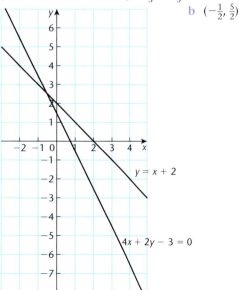

5   Missing values are 17, 9, 5, 9.

6   a   Missing values are 0, -4.5, -4, 8.

   b

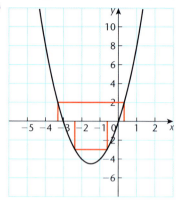

   c   i -3.6 and 0.6

       ii -2.37 and -0.63

   d -4.5

7   a   Missing values are -4, 2, 2.25, 0.

   b

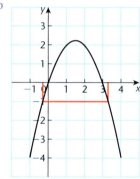

   c -0.30 and 3.30

   d   i 2.25

       ii 1.5

8   a

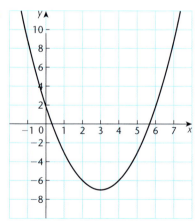

   b   3

Exam practice 9E

1 a

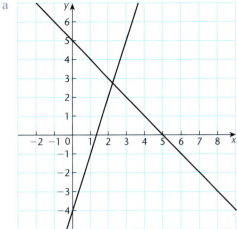

b $x = 2\frac{1}{4}$, $y = 2\frac{3}{4}$

2 a

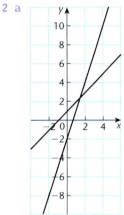

b $x = 1\frac{1}{2}$, $y = 2\frac{1}{2}$

3 a $x^2 - 3x + 5 = -1$ **b** $x^2 - 3x + 5 = 7$
  c $x^2 - 3x + 5 = 15$

4 a -0.5 and 3.5
  b $x^2 - 3x + 5$ rearranges to $x^2 - 3x + 6 = 1$
  and the line $y = 1$ does not cross the curve.

5 a -2.8 and 1.8 **b** -3 and 2
  c -3.2 and 2.2

6 a 0.3 and 1.7 **b** -0.2, 2.2
  c $x = 0$ and 2

Exam practice 9F

1 a

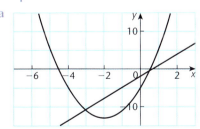

b $\frac{1}{2}$ and -3

2 -2.14 and 0.31

3 a $x^2 + x = 3$
  b $x^2 + x = 2x$
  c $x^2 + x = 2x + 4$
  d $x^2 + x = 3x - 4$

4 a $x^2 + 5x - 6 = 6x - 7$
  b $x^2 + 5x - 6 = 4x - 4$
  c $x^2 + 5x - 6 = 3x - 12$
  d $x^2 + 5x - 6 = -3x - 10$

5 a Draw the graph of $y = 6x - 2$ and see where
  it cuts $y = x^2 + 7x - 2$.
  b Draw the graph of $y = 5x + 9$ and see where
  it cuts $y = x^2 + 7x - 2$.
  c Draw the graph of $y = 7x + 3$ and see where
  it cuts $y = x^2 + 7x - 2$.
  d Draw the graph of $y = x^2 + 7x - 2$ and see
  where it cuts $y = 3$.

6

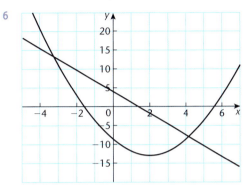

Draw the graph of $y = -3x + 4$ and see where
it cuts $y = x^2 - 4x - 9$.
Solutions are -3.14 and 4.14.

7 a and b

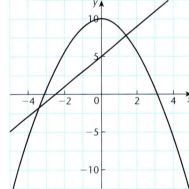

  $x = \pm 3.16$
  c i -3.45 and 1.45
    ii $x^2 + 2x - 5 = 0$

Exam practice 10A

1 a $1 : 4$ **b** $16 : 3$ **c** $4 : 1$ **d** $1 : 3$ **e** $1 : 6$
  f $2 : 1$ **g** $4 : 3$ **h** $1 : 2$ **i** $6 : 5$

2 a $1 : 2 : 3$ **b** $1 : 4 : 3$ **c** $4 : 7 : 3$
  d $4000 : 800 : 1$ **e** $5 : 6 : 3$ **f** $1 : 3 : 10$

3 $3 : 4$

4 a $3 : 2$ **b** $2 : 5$

5 $8 : 12 : 9$

6 a $5 : 8$ **b** $55 : 76$

7 $1 : 80$

8 $1 : 15$

9 $1 : 300\,000$

10 $1 : 200$

Exam practice 10B

1. 18 cm
2. 72 cm
3. 24 m
4. £253.33
5. 37.5 cm
6. 8
7. a $\frac{3}{4}$ cup   b $333\frac{1}{3}$ ml
8. a 40 kg   b 187.5 kg

Exam practice 10C

1. a 42p : 28p   b 24 cm : 40 cm
   c £24 : £30   d £7.50 : £12.50
2. Dave 15 and Tim 25.
3. Molly £30 and Deborah £45.
4. 16
5. 60 m^2
6. 46 g
7. 1.5 m, 3.5 m, 1 m
8. £80, £100, £80
9. 20 litres sand, 25 litres peat, 5 litres fertilizer.
10. $7\frac{3}{11}$ litres
11. 392 ml
12. 571 ml
13. a 283 ml   b 170 ml
14. 2.31 kg
15. a 3 : 4 : 6
    b Mr Peters £1846.15, Mrs Jones £2461.54, Mr Patel £3692.31.
16. a Tom £58.80, Jane £117.60   b £8.40

Exam practice 10D

1. a £10.80   b $\frac{3}{4}$ unit   c £7.92
2. a 1.5p   b 40 minutes
3. 3 hours
4. a 7.5 units   b 8 hours
5. £70
6. £655 (3 s.f.)
7. 500
8. 8.1×10^6
9. 15 volts
10. 0.15 kg
11. 70 km/h
12. £5.265, £5.27

Exam practice 10E

1. 12
2. 40
3. 32
4. 4
5. £400

Exam practice 10F

1. $y = 4x^2$
2. $V = \dfrac{112.5}{l^2}$
3. $R = \frac{17}{30}\sqrt{A}$

4. a $t = \frac{1}{2}(s^2 + 1)$ b i 1.22   ii 7
5. a $y = \dfrac{36}{\sqrt{x}}$ b i 51.84   ii $\frac{36}{7}$
6. a $n = \dfrac{4500}{x^2}$ b 45
7. a $V = \dfrac{2h^3}{45}$ b 1200 ml
8. a 432   b 5
9. 1
10. 17.68 mph (2 d.p.)
11. £18075
12. 240 litres per hour

Exam practice 10G

1. A
2. a C   b D
3. a $p = \dfrac{2n}{3}$ b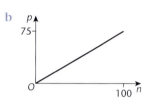
4. a $t = \dfrac{40}{v}$
   b Missing values are 80, 20, 10.
   c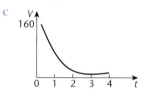

Examination practice paper

Section A

1. a 2.378082192   b 2.38
2. a 630 ml   b 125 ml
3. a £8.67   b 30%
4. a $48 = 2^4 \times 3$ b 12   c 60
5. $5.9 \times 10^7 = 59\,000\,000$ is > 50 million
6. £4.68
7. a $V = 20h$ b 28 m^3
8. 50

Section B

1. 36 mph
2. 5 pints
3. a 857 750   b 2350
4. 40 litres
5. a $\frac{3}{20}$ b 5   c 3^6 d $\frac{1}{7}$
6. 484
7. 0.553
8. a -2 b 4.5, -1.5
9. a $\sqrt{27} + \sqrt{12} - \sqrt{3} = \sqrt{9 \times 3} + \sqrt{4 \times 3} - \sqrt{3}$
   $$= 3\sqrt{3} + 2\sqrt{3} - \sqrt{3}$$
   $$= 4\sqrt{3}$$
   b $\frac{1}{48}$

Index